AF353784

# Spiritual Dimensions of Eye Floaters

A Seer's View, Open Eye Meditation, Ecstasy, Carlos Castaneda, Near-Death Experiences

**Floco Tausin**

**Leuchtstruktur Verlag**

**ISBN 9783907400913**

Copyright © Leuchtstruktur Verlag / Floco Tausin 2022


**Print:**

**Ingramspark.com**


Further information about the subject of eye floaters:
eye-floaters.info

Weitere Informationen zum Thema Mouches volantes:
mouches-volantes.com

# Contents

# Introduction

In the mid-1990s I met a man named Nestor living in the solitude
of the hilly Emmental region of Switzerland. Nestor has a unique
and provocative claim: that he focuses for years on a constellation
of huge shining spheres and strings which have been formed in his
field of vision. He interprets this phenomenon as a subtle structure
formed by our consciousness which in turn creates our material
world. Nestor, who calls himself a seer, ascribes this subjective
visual perception to his long lasting efforts to develop his consciousness. This includes an appropriate lifestyle as well as practices for both temporary and permanent increase of the intensity of
consciousness. Nestor claims that, through these physical and concentrative practices, his spheres and strings that were at first
small, far away and very mobile, had now enlarged, come closer,
started to shine, and now he could hold them in suspension with
his gaze. There, in the centre of the visual field, there would be
one last sphere, the "source", into which we human beings would
enter when we fall asleep or die. Nestor is convinced that if we get
near this last sphere as much as possible in our lifetime, we have
the chance to enter into it keeping our full consciousness – and
thereby overcome death.

*Core-surround floaters in a seer's view. Source: Floco Tausin.*

## Vitreous opacity or light of consciousness?

I have told the story of my apprenticeship with Nestor in my book Mouches Volantes – *Eye Floaters as Shining Structure of Consciousness* (2009). When I started seeing these dots and strings myself, I did a lot of research. I found out that this subjective visual phenomenon was not only known, but widespread. However, the way it is commonly understood deviates significantly from Nestor's statements. In our culture, the authority to interpret this phenomenon has been with ophthalmology for centuries. There, these dots and strands are known by the term "eye floaters" or *mouches volantes* (French for "flying flies"). Eye floaters are an

8

entoptic appearance, i.e. caused by the human visual system itself. In that case, it's a cloudiness of the vitreous body that affects the patient's vision. This perception is explained by the fact that the vitreous body shrinks and liquefies with increasing age (*synere-sis*). Parts of the vitreous structure consisting of hyaluronic acid and collagen fibrils clump together and cast shadows on the retina, which become visible as scattered mobile dots and strings. Eye floaters are considered harmless. The general medical advice is to ignore them. As a precaution, one may have their eyes examined for a possible retinal detachment. This is especially necessary when the floaters are suddenly accompanied by large dark clouds ("soot rain") and lightning.

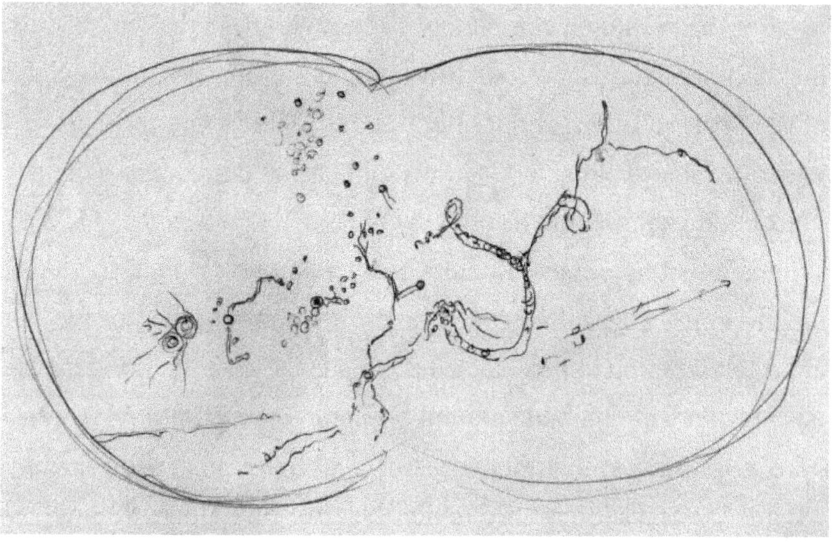

*Common eye floaters. Source: Floco Tausin.*

Many people can see their floaters if they pay attention. To most, they are just a curiosity and not really distracting. Some people, however, feel disturbed by their dots and strands, such that they are considering surgical measures. Vitrectomy, for example, removes parts of the vitreous humour. Laser vitreolysis, on the other hand, attempts to break up single floater strands through fast laser pulses. However, such treatments are risky and are not recommended by most ophthalmologists to remove the harmless eye floaters.

So, are eye floaters vitreous opacities, or are they the light of consciousness? Nestor has identified eye floaters as the first appearance of what he calls "shining structure" or "luminous spheres" and "luminous strings" and understands as the light of consciousness. If he is right, then the ophthalmological understanding of eye floaters would be completely wrong. How can that be? Fact is that ophthalmologists cannot always find the floaters in the eyes of their patients. This is not only true for looking into the eyes with a slit lamp, but also for more sophisticated methods such as ultrasound examination or optical coherence tomography (OCT). Why is it that not all eye floaters can be objectively located? Ophthalmologists assert that some floaters are just too small or too close to the retina to be detected. If this is the case, then the methods and devices available are not efficient enough until now. Another possibility is that there are different types of subjective visual phenomena summarized under the term "eye floaters", and that one of them is not a vitreous opacity. Even if actual vitreous opacities and the first appearances of the shining structure look similar at first glance, there are clear differences on closer inspection. The former are rather described and depicted as something dark and blurred, like shadows, streaks or spots. The latter, on the other hand, are scattered transparent or luminous dots and strands with clear contours. The dots contain a core, and the strands are filled with dots. The former can be detected and treated, the latter cannot – simply because they are no vitreous opacities. I suggest understanding the shining dots and strands, just like the entoptic phenomena of phosphenes or form constants, as a visual expression of certain states of the nervous system. Then Nestor's assertion would no longer be out of question that it is our consciousness intensity that transforms the small, mobile, and transparent dots and strands – the eye floaters – into big and stable shining spheres and tubes.

*Eye Floaters. Source: Floco Tausin.*

## Tracing the shining structure

For years I have tried to understand in theory and practice what Nestor has taught me about the shining structure. Though I cannot confirm all of his claims by my previous experience, I have seen enough of the shining structure to dismiss the ideas of "vitreous cloudiness" and "clumped vitreous fibrils". I have come to realize that these dots and strings are in fact a phenomenon of consciousness that can be intensified in luminosity and size. What exactly this means and where it leads – for example, whether there is a centre with an exit in this shining structure, as Nestor claims – I try to find out.

This collection of previously published and revised texts is part of this endeavour. In these texts, I consider the spiritual dimensions of eye floaters: what observations speak for eye floaters as the light of consciousness and therefore as a potential spiritual phenomenon? How can this consciousness phenomenon be used for spiritual practices? And what further spiritual practices or worldviews could have been inspired by eye floaters? The first chapter, *Floating Spheres and Strings in a Seer's View*, describes Nestor's perception and understanding of eye floaters. According to Nestor, eye floaters are the shining structure of consciousness that can be used as an object of concentration. In addition, eye floaters also reflect our present intensity of consciousness, and they provide an exit from our earthly existence. *Open Eye Meditation* discusses material and subtle meditation objects to develop the "inner sense". The four stages of meditation according to Patanjali's eight-limbed yoga can be used to guide the open eye meditation and are exemplified by the shining structure floaters. The third chapter, *Ecstasy – Hair Standing on End*, is about a phenomenon that we know as chills or goose bumps in certain emotional states, and that has its place in love and sexuality, music, poetry and spirituality of various cultures. It has also its place on the path in the shining structure according to Nestor: when large amounts of energy flow out of the body – a state called "ecstasy" – the spheres and strings of the shining structure move closer and light up. In such moments, we approach our source in the structure. The fourth and fifth chapters deal with spiritual practices and views that could have been inspired by eye floaters. *Eye Floaters as a Source of Inspiration for Carlos Castaneda* discusses, as the title indicates, whether – and to what extent – eye floaters could have been critical to cult author Carlos Castaneda when developing the spiritual world of Yaqui Indian Don Juan. And finally *Eye Floaters and Near-Death Experiences* assumes that near-death experiences – and thus our ideas of what will happen when we die – are characterized by the visionary experience of the shining structure. The thesis of this article is that floaters and other entoptic phenomena are phenomena of consciousness which continue to exist in states of near-death – and possibly even beyond death.

# 1

## Floating spheres and strings in a seer's view

**First published:**
Tausin, Floco (2010): "Eye Floaters. Floating spheres and strings in a seer's view". Source: Link[1].

In anthropology and psychology it has been known for some time that altered states of consciousness promote the perception of subjective visual phenomena, i.e. hallucinations on the one hand, and so-called entoptic phenomena on the other (Tausin 2006). Entoptic phenomena are luminous moving geometric shapes that occur frequently in states of trance. Since entoptics are physiologically associated with specific states of the visual nervous system, they count as culturally independent universal phenomena of humanity (Lewis-Williams/Dowson 1988; Thurston 1991). Shamans, druids, seers, holy women and men of the past and contemporary societies and traditions have seen such patterns during ritual ceremonies and have interpreted them in accordance with their worldview.

**Floaters**

One of these people is the hermit Nestor whom I met in the mid-1990s in the Swiss Emmental (Tausin 2009a). Through his consciousness development, Nestor encountered a certain type of entoptic phenomena which he has taken as a meditation object and has developed for years. The phenomenon in question is the simple geometric shapes, i.e. transparent or luminous  spheres and strings. While the spheres are often seen as concentric circles, the strings partially consist of rows of spheres. These spheres and strings move across the visual field at variable speeds, usually downwards, but they can be influenced by eye movements. In ophthalmology, this phenomenon has long been known as 'eye floaters' (French/German: *mouches volantes*, Latin: *muscae volitantes*). 'Floaters' is a general term for all possible opacities in the vitreous body. But the floaters at issue are considered as 'idiopathic', i.e. without pathological cause – age-related and harmless, so to speak. The explanations vary between remaining embryonic stem cells, cell debris between the retina and the vitreous body, and hyaluronic vitreous fibrils clumped together due to vitreous liquefaction and posterior vitreous detachment (Trick 2007; Sendrowski/Bronstein 2010). Often, floaters can't be seen and effectively treated by ophthalmologists (Tausin 2009c).

*Shining structure floaters. Source: Floco Tausin.*

## Nestor's teaching: the shining structure of consciousness and the inner sense

Nestor's statements about eye floaters differ significantly from the ophthalmologic explanation. To him, these spheres and strings emerged from consciousness. They form a coherent structure on which we project our material world like on a screen. They are directly connected with our will. And ultimately, our pure egoless consciousness fits into one such sphere in this structure.

Whether our eye floaters have a material counterpart in the eye (or the brain) is irrelevant to Nestor. For him, we see these spheres and strings not with our eyes but with an "inner sense" or the "third eye", as he sometimes calls it. He characterizes this inner sense as an eye that gradually opens up through the withdrawal of the external senses as experienced in concentration exercises. Therefore, initial symptoms of eye floaters indicate the beginning of the opening of the third eye. The degree of openness of the third eye depends on the average consciousness of a society of a given time and culture, but also on individual efforts. The fact that many people see floaters in our contemporary Western societies means, according to Nestor, that many people already have a connection to their inner sense – even if they don't work with it consciously.

With such statements, Nestor ascribes an extraordinary meaning to the visual phenomena called "floaters": they are a spiritual phenomenon, and thus a directly perceptible starting point for our own spiritual development, for the realization of the world and of our true selves. But what made Nestor utter such claims? First, he emphasizes that his statements about the spheres and strings are grounded in his own seeing. In this regard, it is important to understand that his description of the spheres  and strings differs from the one of most other people. He doesn't see isolated small dots  and strings that drift  away permanently,  but large,  bright spheres and tubes which he is able to hold in suspension and, therefore, to see clearly. His claim to deal with what is commonly called "floaters" is based on his experience of the transformation of the small movable dots and strings into large spheres and tubes.


## The zoom effect and the layers of consciousness

According to Nestor, this transformation is connected to his consciousness development  which, in turn, results  from a specific lifestyle,  including  an  ethical  attitude,  a  natural  and  balanced vegetarian and vegan diet, physical exercises, breathing exercises, concentration  and  meditation  practices,  as well  as  ritually  altered states of consciousness. This way of life leads to the accumulation of energy and to the opening up of the body. This means that a seer is no longer forced to give off his energy solely through bodily and mental actions, but is able to release it directly as a relaxing prickle or ecstasy into the environment.

If this  energy  release  is  intense  enough, the  visual  perception changes: in the moment of ecstasy, an object perceived shines up and "zooms in" abruptly. Thus, the visual field of a seer (the "picture") shows less of the world, but the objects looked at appear bigger, more focused, luminous and colourful. This observation is the reason for Nestor to assume that our visual system consists of several "layers" lined up one after another on which those processes are enacted that we collectively call "our world". Each layer corresponds to a specific state of consciousness, showing each time the same "world", which is, however, seen and experienced very differently. Basically, human beings are able to experience the whole spectrum of consciousness, but because of our education our focus is fixed on a single layer, shared by most people. The lifestyle and the bodily and mental exercises of a seer dissolve this fixation and allows for a penetration of these layers. Any individual capable of changing his or her visual perception and consciousness by focusing on unfamiliar layers is, in Nestor's term, a "seer".

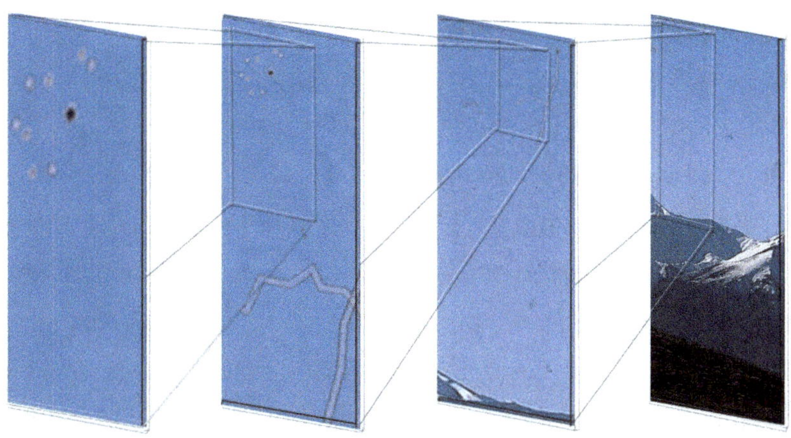

*Floaters, zoom effect and the layers of consciousness. Source: Floco Tausin.*

The process of "seeing" is goal-oriented insofar as the seer acts to increase his energy metabolism both, in the short term and in the longer term to bring about more intense states of consciousness and to see the "picture" closer and more detailed. This process is experienced as a forward movement within the shining structure. This means that a seer, gradually or abruptly, penetrates the layers of consciousness, and, in the long term, that he focuses on new spheres that appear in the upper and rear part of the "picture". Nestor calls this spiritual and visual forward movement "the path in the shining structure".

## The constellation of spheres and the "source"

The path in the shining structure is a path of reduction: in the beginning we see a large quantity of dots and strings which move before our eyes without any recognizable order or obvious meaning. After the "leap into the left side of consciousness", i.e. the first ecstasy of a human being that releases a great amount of energy and zooms in the picture and the structure to a large extent, the spheres of a seer become increasingly less but bigger. The seer recognizes that his spheres are arranged in a constellation revealing fundamental principles that we find in both, nature and culture.

Besides this constellation there's a second phenomenon that makes the shining structure meaningful: the "beginning of being" or "source". It's a sphere at the end of the path in the shining structure. According to Nestor, this is the sphere into which we enter, both when we fall asleep and when we die. Entering into this sphere means to become one with the structure, and therefore to become one with the whole picture. Nestor's path is thus a mystical path: the seers believe that we lost the primordial unity with the picture in the process of embodiment and of becoming individual and separate personalities. The way in the shining structure leads back to this unity. The intention of a seer is to approach this last sphere and, if possible, to enter it consciously – before or during physical death.

## The importance of floaters

As with all mysticism and religion, Nestor's teaching is a set of statements based on subjective perceptions and experiences. The only way of testing these statements is to have our own personal and subjective experiences with "seeing". What a seer like Nestor gives us for everyday life is a sense of being connected with a picture that structures the processes we call "life" or "world". This connection manifests in an early stage in so-called eye floaters, the dots and strings floating before our eyes. With these shining structure floaters, Nestor gives us something immediate, visible and individual for our consciousness development – a phenomenon we can use independent of external objects for daily concentration and meditation (Tausin 2009b).

# References


Lewis-Williams, J. D.; Dowson, T. A. (1988): "The Signs of All Times: Entoptic Phenomena in Upper Paleolithic Art". *Current Anthropology 29*, no. 2: 201-245

Sendrowski, David P.; Bronstein, Mark A. (2010): "Current treatment for vitreous floaters". *Optometry 81*: 157-161

Tausin, Floco (2009a): *Mouches Volantes. Eye Floaters as Shining Structure of Consciousness.* Bern: Leuchtstruktur Verlag

Tausin, Floco (2009b): "Open Eye Meditation. The visual way to the development of the inner sense". *The International Journal of Healing and Caring (IJHC) 9*, no. 3. wholistichealingresearch.com/ijhchome (28.8.09)

Tausin, Floco (2009c): "Mouches volantes nicht im Glaskörper?" *Ganzheitlich Sehen 4/09.* mouches-volantes.com/news/newsdezember2009.htm#2 (12.9.22)

Tausin, Floco. (2006). "Mouches volantes und Trance. Ein universelles Phänomen bei erweiterten Bewusstseinszuständen früher und heute". *Jenseits des Irdischen 3*

Thurston, Linda (1991): Entoptic Imagery in People and Their Art (*M.A. thesis, 1991, web edition 1997*). home.comcast.net/~markk2000/thurston/thesis.html (2011)

Trick, Gary L.; Kronenberg, Alaina (2007): "Entoptic Imagery and Afterimages". *Duane's Ophthalmology,* ed. by William Tasman and Edward A. Jaeger. Philadelphia: Lippincott Williams & Wilkins


## Links


Link[1]: *Holistic Vision 2*. eye-floaters.info/news/news-june2010.htm#1 (12.9.22)

# 2

## Open Eye Meditation

**First published:**

Tausin, Floco (2009): "Open Eye Meditation. The visual way to the development of the inner sense". Source: Link[1].

Delicately chiselled features and grey concrete blocks, monotonous traffic noise and resounding laughter, scratchy cigarette smoke and irritant perfume, sweet baklava and hot samosas, soft pillows and hard benches – what we know as our weekday is a tide of miscellaneous information which we receive with our five senses and put together to an integral picture in the brain. The sense organs are the gates of our body – they connect the outside world with the inner world and determine, dependent on our state of consciousness, how we experience this world.

No wonder, the spiritually awake individuals in the East and the West always paid great attention to their senses. Indian philosophers, for example, studied the interplay of sense organs, sense objects, thinking and consciousness very extensively. They concluded that an unbridled sense activity is an obstacle on the way to the realization of the self or God. It is said in the Bhagavadgita:

"O son of Kunti, the senses are so strong and impetuous that they forcibly carry away the mind even of a man of discrimination who is endeavoring to control them" (2.60).

Sensual pleasure is regarded as deceitful because it "appears like nectar at first but poison at the end … it is said to be the nature of passion" (18.38). Does this mean now that we should shut the eyes and stop the ears up if we try to lead a more spiritual and conscious life? Of course not, it's rather about making the sensual activity useful for the consciousness development as well. To achieve this, the wise men and women of earlier times have given us a wonderful instrument: meditation.

In modern societies, meditation is often taught apart from a specific religion, partly as a therapeutic remedy for stress, strain, emotional problems etc. Practicing meditation will undoubtedly calm down our sense activity time and again and counteract an overstimulation of our sense organs, making us restless and dissatisfied. But meditation goes beyond a therapeutic application. It is a means to a higher end, a step that should lead to more: the practitioner tries to gain knowledge of the world and of her- or himself which is clear from thoughts and feelings.

## The inner sense

We can assume that such subtle knowledge takes place by the connection of a subtle sense organ with a subtle sense object. According to my teacher Nestor, I call this subtle sense "inner sense". Nestor does not understand this inner sense as a sixth sense but as a combination of all five senses. The inner sense, therefore, is immediately related to the physical senses, which are internalized by it (Tausin 2009).

*The cosmic eye between the eyebrows of the Buddha. Source: Link[2].*

In many cultures and religions, we find the notion of an inner sense, thought of as a mode of perception which directly and intuitively gives insight to the essence or true nature of the object perceived. Often this subtle or inner sense is linked to the eye as a widespread symbol of light, cognition and truth. It is then addressed as the "inner eye", "third eye" or "eye of the heart", common among mystics who experienced the divine light. In Indian mythology, for example, this inner sense is expressed as god Shiva's frontal eye that gives him unifying vision. Accordingly, tantric yogis try to open this third eye by activating the "Ajna Chakra", located between the eyebrows. Likewise, the Buddha Siddhartha Gautama received enlightenment through a "celestial eye" (Pali: *dibbacakkhu*), which permitted him to understand the forces of existence and their manifestation in the chain of causality (Gonda 1969; Meslin 2005; Ramen 2008).

The Greek philosophers spoke of an "Eye of the Spirit" which has to be opened and purified to see the truth (Hansen 1998; Scheerer 2007). While the Old Testament calls the prophets "seers" and refers to an all-seeing eye or "Eye of Providence" that turns to those who fear God and gives them superior insights or strength (Meslin 2005), the New Testament takes up the Greek philosopher's notion of the "Eye of the Soul or Heart": the eye becomes the object of purity (Matthew 6.22), and the Eye of the Heart has to be opened in order to see God (Acts 9.18, Rom 1.19). Likewise, the Muslim mystics, the Sufis, identified the "eye of the heart" (Arabian: '*ayn al-qalb*; Persian: *chishm-i dil*) with the imminent intellect. The famous Persian poet Hatif writes:

"Open the 'eye of the heart' so that thou canst see the spirit / And gain vision of that which visible is not" (Nasr 2006).

Over the centuries, Desert Fathers, Gnostics, and Mystics alike further reported experiences of the inner sense as an inner eye or eye of the heart or soul. Since the early modern period, Western esoterics and scientists interested in unifying the scientific and spiritual traditions are trying to find a physiological correspondence of this inner sense. In recent years, for example, the inner sense has been associated with the pineal gland, based on scientific insights about the light sensitivity of this gland (Gonda 1969; Crystal 2009; Eggetsberger 2009).

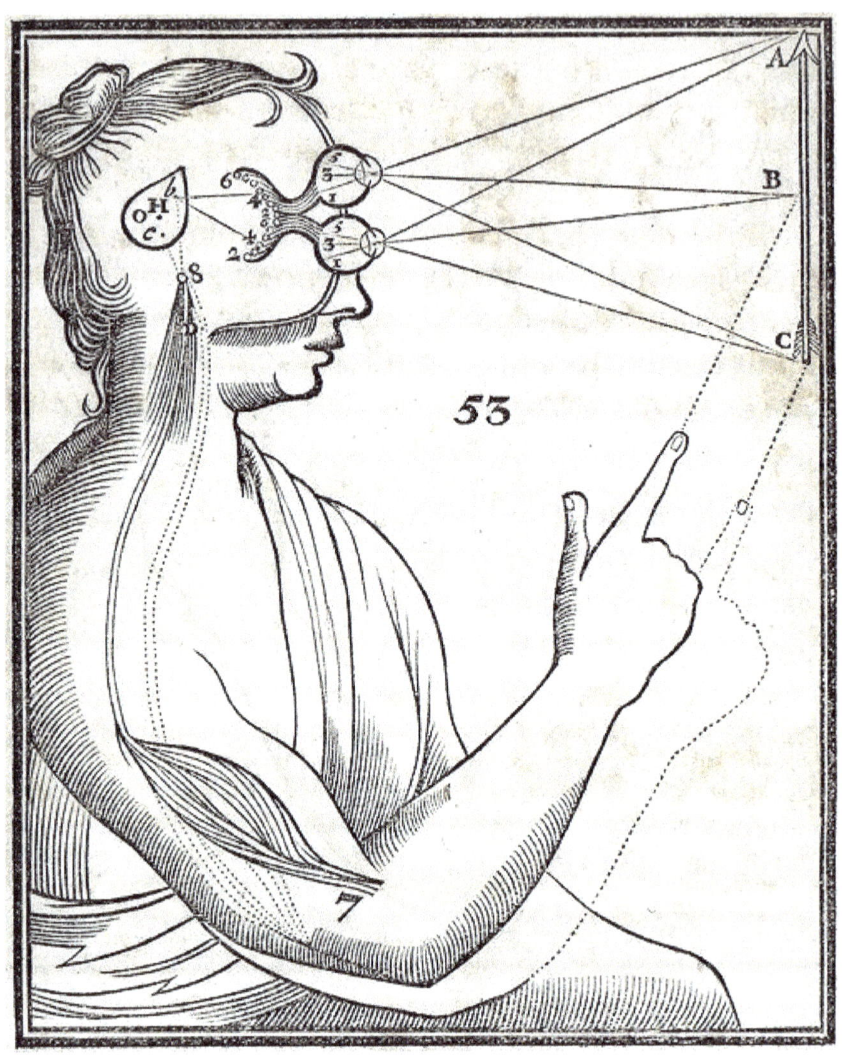


The relation between perception, soul and pineal gland after René Descartes (1596-1650). Source: Link[3].

## Meditation for the development of the inner sense

While meditating, many of us have come to know first aspects of an inner sense awakening, for example, subjective visual appearances, ecstatic feelings or intuitive insights. But if we want to develop that inner sense to its full bloom, years and decades of constant exercise are necessary. Anyone of us ready to practice should choose a meditation method that works directly with the inner sense or with its objects and function (cp. Lehnert 2009).

A good starting point for such a meditation can be found in the *Yoga Sutras* of the Indian philosopher Patanjali (2nd c. BCE). His eight-limbed path deals first with an ethical lifestyle as well as body and breathing exercises. These exercises lead to intellectual and physical balance – prerequisites for a successful meditation. The four stages of meditation succeeding one another are: withdrawing the senses (Sanskrit: *pratyahara*), concentration (*dharana*), meditation (*dhyana*) and absorption or contemplation (*samadhi*). This meditation can be carried out on material or subtle objects (Desikachar 1997; Venkatesananda 2009).

## Material meditation objects

Material meditation objects are perceived through the eyes, not through the inner sense, but concentrating on them can lead to awareness of subtle aspects. Meditation on material objects should support the inner sense or third eye in its function to mediate between the right and left brain hemispheres, or the two sides of consciousness, combined. It should make aware to us our right intuitive emotional side as well as our left analytical rational side, bringing them into harmony with each other. This may be most readily experienced by means of squinting techniques which have been developed likewise in Western and Eastern traditions. Two different types of squinting must be distinguished here, though: the letting go of the eyes (parallel viewing) in which the concentration point shifts behind the object looked at, and the concentrative directing inside the eyes (cross viewing) in which the concentration point is drawn in front of the object looked at, in the direction of the observer (Wieser 2009; Cooper 2009). The second type, which I call 'doubling', is the type of squinting ideal for meditation (Tausin 2009).

The simplest exercise of doubling is looking at the root of the nose, in the tradition of Indian yogis. However, doubling can also be applied to distant material objects. Anthropologist and author Carlos Castaneda (1972, 1977; Tausin 2006a), for example, mentions a seeing technology called "gazing", which at first means to focus the view on an object, similar to the hatha yogi's cleaning exercise *trataka* (Gheranda-Samhita 1.53-54; Hathayogapradipika 2.31). Sometimes, though, it is combined with squinting, in which the practitioner moves apart the two pictures and thus superimposes two equally formed objects. The concentration on this superimposed object synchronizes the two sides of consciousness or brain hemispheres and, regularly practiced, produces a depth perception that carries the practitioner into other spheres of consciousness (Castaneda 1972, 1977).

Another example of this form of meditation is the meditation on the "Tables of Chartres". The tables are three legendary geometric figures of equal surface area, made from red and blue coloured metal pieces, shaped as rectangle, square, and circle. They are put down before oneself in two rows of alternating colour and shape and doubled until a superimposed third table group appears in the middle. The knowledge around this old meditation type was maintained and passed on by Romani people and published by the French author Pierre Derlon (Derlon 1978; Pennington 2002, 2009).

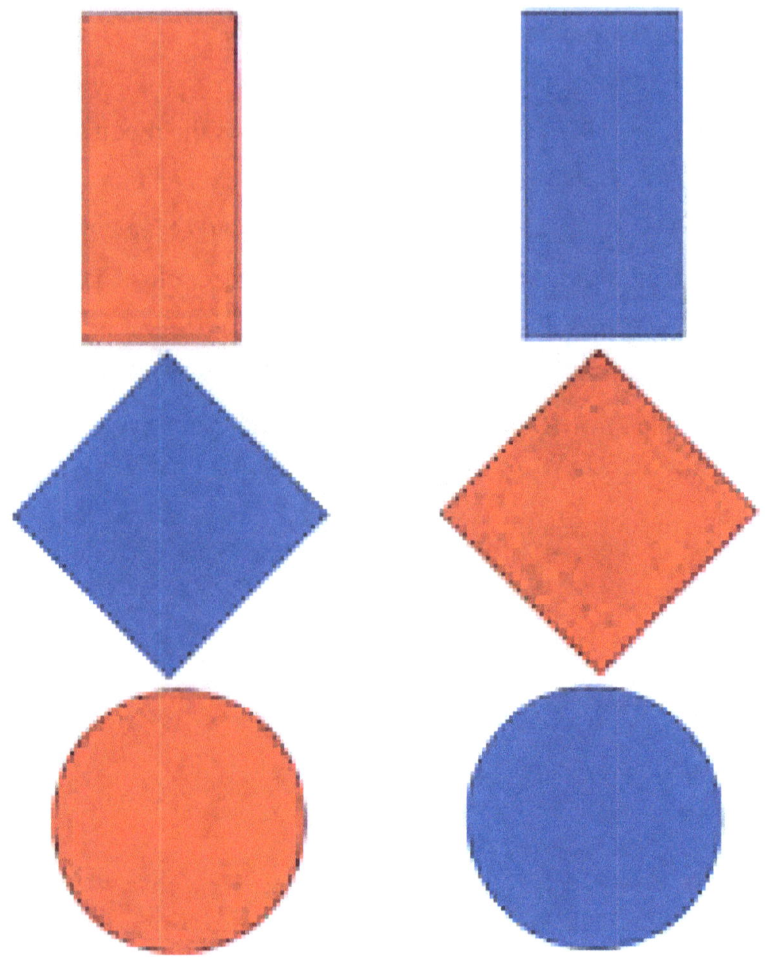

*The Tables of Chartres. Source: Link[4].*

**The subtle objects: Subjective visual phenomena**

Subtle meditation objects for focus can be emotions, sensations (Shaw 2006; Sayadaw 2009) and thoughts (Underwood 2005). For developing the inner sense, however, there are objects that are particularly well suited for meditation, which appear through the fusion of the inner sense and the visual sense. I'm referring to those subjective visual phenomena that are known in ophthalmology as "entoptic phenomena" or "entoptics". Entoptic phenomena are believed by observers to be seen outside of themselves. Physiologically explained, however, they are generated by the observer's neurophysiological visual system. Included are contrasting coloured afterimages, coloured spots and blurs in the dark (phosphenes), fast moving starlets flashing up (blue field entoptic phenomenon), mobile and scattered semi-transparent dots strands (eye floaters or *mouches volantes*) as well as geometric structures which appear in consciousness states altered by ecstasy techniques (form constants) (Chen et al. 2009; Sinclair et al. 1989; Tausin 2006b; Trick/Kronenberg 2007). Such entoptics were watched by people throughout recent recorded history, often provided with religious meanings and used as concentration objects (Lewis-Williams/Dowson 1988; Tausin 2006c). The geometric patterns in the artwork of present and past societies that include consciousness altering practices and trance, for example, testify to this (Thurston 1997).

*An entoptic phenomena suitable for meditation: shining structure floaters. Source: Floco Tausin.*


## Meditation on mobile dots and strands (eye floaters)

The four stages of meditation according to the Indian philosopher Patanjali shall be explained now with one of these subjective visual phenomena: the mobile, transparent dots and strands which often float in our field of vision and tend to drift away the moment we try to look at them. Many of us already became aware of them once in a while, and most people don't mind, but some are actually concerned about their dots and strands. In ophthalmology this phenomenon is regarded as a harmless kind of vitreous opacity and called "eye floaters" or "muscae volitantes". Sometimes the term "floaters" is used to designate all kinds of vitreous opacities, while "muscae volitantes" (Latin for "flying flies") or its French equivalent "mouches volantes" describe the specific type of harmless floaters referred to above.

Seeing floaters provides a first-class meditation object to work with: these dots and strands form an individual pattern with each of us and therefore are an unmistakable expression of ourselves, like a thumbprint. We do not need to remind ourselves to carry them with us and can meditate on them whenever and wherever we feel like it. A powerful look upwards suffices to bring them to our awareness and hold them in our visual field. Moreover, the meditation on our dots and strands is an open eye meditation, which has the advantage to keep us awake and to provide us with the energy of daylight (cp. Tsung-tse 2009).

The first of the four limbs (Sanskrit: *anga*) of the process of meditation in the system of Patanjali is withdrawing the senses. This means that we bring the objects of the inner sense, the dots and strands, into our field of vision and consciously look at them. Doing that, we withdraw our five senses from the material sense objects of the outer world and channel the energy usually needed to maintain our sensory functioning to the inner sense. In this first step we explore our dots and strands, get to know their forms, constellations and movements, see that there are different dots and strands in the left and the right eye or in the left and the right side of the brain, respectively, and we may then elect either to concentrate on the one or the other side at any particular moment.

We notice that it is not easy to see these dots and strands because they constantly drift away, mainly downward. Only by realignment of our gaze are we able to keep them in the field of vision. What we have here is a direct bodily-visual expression of what Patanjali calls *vrittis* – subtle waves or mental fluctuations which represent our mental reaction to stimuli from outside or inside. These waves prevent us from longer concentration because they produce impressions (Sanskrit: *samskara*) in our consciousness, which in turn react to further stimuli. This realignment (also called fluctuation or modification in the Indian philosophy) takes place at different levels: every new thought, every feeling, every alignment of our gaze means an ending and new beginning of concentration. Thus, the meditation on our dots and strands always shows us how deep our concentration already is.

With increasing experience in seeing the objects of the inner sense, we reach the second step or limb, which is concentration. We will realize that we can hold these dots and strands in the visual field more easily and longer, and that they gradually get smaller, sharper and more shining. In several verses of his *Yoga Sutras,* Patanjali, too, mentions the perceivable increase of a radiant light during meditation that would, taken as a concentration object, lead to the knowledge of the subtle realms. This light can be seen directly in these dots and strands, and that's why Nestor (Tausin 2009) speaks of eye floaters as a "shining structure of consciousness".

If we manage to hold the dots and strands in suspension for some time, without realignment of the look, we have reached the third stage, the actual meditation. The dots only float a little and shine clearly. Our attention is now uninterruptedly focused on the dots and strands of the right or left side; our inner sense dominates and the five physiological senses fade from conscious awareness.

Our five senses rest completely in the last step, contemplation. The inner sense has woken up completely and lets us recognize and feel immediately and with great intensity the true significance of these balls and strands and their relation to ourselves. In Indian philosophy, this contemplative knowledge has a mystical quality insofar as the seer becomes one with the seen and thereby experiences the liberating knowledge of his true self.

**In summary**

To develop the inner sense or third eye, squinting techniques and the concentration on subtle objects, considered as objects of this inner sense, are suitable. The open eye meditation on so-called entoptic phenomena is a concentrative and "cataphatic" meditation method (Underwood 2005) insofar as it is aimed at the production and holding of inner images. At the same time, it is approaching the "apophatic" insight meditation forms, aspiring to dissolve all consciousness contents. The appearance of abstract entoptics can be regarded as a result of the dissolution of concrete mental images and thoughts (Tausin 2009).

A holistic investigation on entoptics is beyond the usual reduction of these phenomena to their neurophysiological dimensions, as understood by Western medicine. On the one hand, the connection of entoptics to alternate consciousness states, as well as their suitability for higher insights, must be explored and elucidated by subjective comprehension, as with other meditative experiences and other subjective phenomena. On the other hand, humanistic research should refurbish the reception of such subtle phenomena in the different cultures and spiritual traditions. Understanding how other societies and traditions integrate entoptics in their spirituality, arts and everyday life provides us with new insights about the meaning of these phenomena so near, yet unknown, to mankind. By this expansion of the one-sided Western medical perspective, which is largely focused only on physical phenomena and particularly on those that can be measured objectively, we can offer alternative thinking and action options to people who suffer from such subjective perceptions. This new way of dealing with these phenomena offers people the alternative to view and experience them as normal and helpful rather than as pathological, since they are outside the explanatory systems of conventional medicine.

# References

Castaneda, Carlos (1972): *Journey to Ixtlan*. New York: Simon and Schuster

Castaneda, Carlos (1977): *The Second Ring of Power*. New York: Simon and Schuster

Chen, Spencer C. et al. (2009): "Simulating prosthetic vision: I. Visual models of phosphenes". *Vision Research* 49, no. 12: 1493-1506

Cooper, Rachel: "The Logical Approach to Seeing 3D Pictures". *Vision3d.com*. vision3d.com/3views.html (14.10.19)

Crystal, Ellie: "Third Eye – Pineal Gland". *Crystalinks.com*. crystalinks.com/thirdeyepineal.html (13.9.22)

Derlon, Pierre (1978): *Die Gärten der Einweihung*, Basel: Sphinx Verlag

Desikachar, T. K. V. (1997): *Yoga – Tradition und Erfahrung: Die Praxis des Yoga nach dem Yoga Sutra des Patañjali.* Petersberg: Via Nova

Eggetsberger, Gerhard H.: "Gold aktiviert die Zirbeldrüse". *Ipn.at*. ipn.at/ipn.asp?ALH (13.9.22)

Gonda, Jan (1969): *Eye and Gaze in the Veda* (Verhandelingen der Koninklijke Nederlandse Akademie van Wetenschappen. Afdeling Letterkunde. Nieuwe Reeks, Deel *75*). Amsterdam

Hansen, Frank-Peter (1998): *Philosophie von Platon bis Nietzsche* (Digitale Bibliothek, Bd. 2), Berlin: Directmedia

Lehnert, Ralf: "Die Dritte-Auge-Meditation". *Home.arcor.de*. home.arcor.de/ralflehnert/id53.htm (31.7.09)

Lewis-Williams, J. D.; Dowson, T. A. (1988): "The Signs of All Times: Entoptic Phenomena in Upper Paleolithic Art". *Current Anthropology 29*, no. 2: 201-245

Mallinson, James (2004): *The Gheranda Samhita. The original Sanskrit / Gheranda*, translated by James Mallinson, Woodstock: YogaVidya.com

Meslin, Michel (2005): "Eye". *The Encyclopaedia of Religion* (2nd ed.), ed. by Mircea Eliade. Macmillan Reference: 2.939-2.941

Nasr, Seyyed Hossein (2006): *Islamic philosophy from ist origin to the present. Philosophy in the land of prophecy.* Albany: State University of New York Press

Pennington, George (2002): *Die Tafeln von Chartres. Die gnostische Schau des Westens.* Patmos

Pennington, George: "The Tables of Chartres Cathedral". *Pennington-training.com.* pennington-training.com/meditation/tablebook1.pdf (31.7.09)

Ramen, Fred (2008): *Indian Mythology.* New York: Rosen Pub. Group

Sayadaw, Mahasi (n/a): *Practical Vipassana Exercises* (Buddha Dharma Education Association). buddhanet.net/pdf_file/mahasit1.pdf (13.9.22)

Scheerer, E. (2007): "Sinne". *Historisches Wörterbuch der Philosophie 9,* ed. by Joachim Ritter et al. Berlin: Directmedia: 824-869

Shaw, Sarah (2006): Buddhist Meditation. *An anthology of texts from the Pali canon.* London/NY: Routledge

S. H. Sinclair; M. Azar-Cavanaugh; K.A. Soper; R.F. Tuma, and H.N. Mayrovitz (1989): "Investigation of the source of the blue field entoptic phenomenon". *Investigative Ophthalmology and Visual Science* 4: 668-673

Svatmarama, Swami (1914): *Hathayogapradipika. English & Sanskrit,* translated by Pancham Sinh. sacred-texts.com/hin/hyp/index.htm (13.9.22)

Tausin, Floco (2010): *Mouches Volantes. Die Leuchtstruktur des Bewusstseins.* Bern: Leuchtstruktur Verlag

Tausin, Floco (2006a): "Kokons und Fasern – Leuchtkugeln und Leuchtfäden. Mouches volantes als Inspirationsquelle für Carlos Castaneda?" *AHA Magazin* 5

Tausin, Floco (2006b): "Zwischen Innenwelt und Aussenwelt. Entoptische Phänomene und ihre Bedeutung für Bewusstseinsentwicklung und Spiritualität". *Schlangentanz* 3

Thurston, Linda: Entoptic Imagery in People and Their Art, (M.A. thesis, 1991), *webedition 1997,* home.comcast.net/~markk2000/thurston/thesis.html (24.8.09)

Trick, Gary L.; Kronenberg, Alaina (2007): "Entoptic Imagery and Afterimages" *Duane's Ophthalmology*, ed. by William Tasman and Edward A. Jaeger. Philadelphia: Lippincott Williams & Wilkins [electronic edition]

Tsung-tse, Ch'ang-lu (n/a): *Ch'an-yüan ch'ing-kuei Tso-ch'an I.* zensplitter.de/Texte/Tsung-tse/tsung-tse.html (31.7.09)

Underwood, Frederic B. (2005): "Meditation". *The Encyclopaedia of Religion (2nd ed.)*, ed. by Mircea Eliade. Macmillan Reference: 5.816-5.822

Venkatesananda, Swami (n/a): *The Yoga Sutras. Patanjali's Vision of Oneness* (An Interpretative Translation by Swami Venkatesananda). dailyreadings.com/sutras_1.htm (31.7.09)

Wieser, Wolfgang (n/a): "Parallel/cross-eyed 3d view". *Triplespark.net.* triplespark.net/render/stereo/pview.html (13.9.22)

## Links

Link[1]: *The International Journal of Healing and Caring (IJHC) 9*, no. 3. wholistichealingresearch.com/ijhchome (28.8.09)

Link[2]: flickr.com/photos/ddjang/3270103367/ (13.9.22)

Link[3]:
https://blogs.publico.es/alberto-sicilia/files/2021/10/353d8b20e154fd856de668 440bda49b9.jpeg (13.9.22)

Link[4]: pennington-training.com/index.php? option=com_content&view=article&id=10&Itemid=116&lang=de (13.9.22)

# 3

# Ecstasy – Hair Standing on End

**First published:**

Tausin, Floco (2011): "Hair standing on end. Prickle feelings in spirituality and holistic medicine". Source: Link[1].

Many of us experience that prickle feeling with the body hair standing on end and the skin looking like "goose bumps" time and again. It is usually associated or identified with chills, shiver and certain emotional states. Less known, however, is that this prickle is informative and effective in the fields of health care and spirituality. This is suggested by both medical studies and the experience of spiritual masters of different cultures.

## The spiritual significance of the prickle

If the spiritual dimension of the prickle feeling is not immediately evident to us, it may be because our familiar sources of information don't make ties between the two. According to current physiology, goose bumps are a relic of a distant past: when

the hominids of prehistoric times were still covered with dense
hair, the rise of the hair protected from the cold and made women
and men look bigger and more menacing – which is thought to
have helped averting combats in threatening situations. For rela-
tively hairless and clean-shaven modern people, however, the
prickle feeling has become useless. The Bible, on the other hand,
links the phenomenon to fear and terror:

"Fear came upon me, and trembling, which made all my bones to shake.
Then a spirit passed before my face; the hair of my flesh stood up" (Job
4, 14-15).

*Ducks with goose bumps. Source: Link$^2$.*

Religious and spiritual traditions of non-Western cultures point to
a different aspect: prickle feelings are associated with meditative
and ecstatic states, often while experiencing a deep devotional
love towards a deity. This is not so difficult for us to comprehend
if we remember that we know this feeling from very beautiful moments, be it while listening to harmonious music, looking at

touching natural phenomena, or feeling one with a person we love.

Speaking of love and sexuality, the prickle on the skin may be understood as a result of deep and conscious relaxation of body and mind. The *Kamasutra*, a 4th century Indian textbook of carnal love, teaches a particular type of touch that will cause the prickling (Kamasutra 4, 10). Psychologist J. Panksepp observed neurochemical similarities between the prickle feeling and the sexual orgasm – pointing to the fact that the exhilarating prickle is often felt during intense orgasms involving the whole body ("skin orgasm", "full body orgasm").

*Prickling touch according to the* Kamasutra. *Source: Link*[3].

Now we understand the deeper meaning the prickle has for many masters who transformed carnal love into spiritual love: love is not directed to a person, but to God, and the sexual orgasm is replaced by the whole body orgasm of an overwhelming and ecstatic prickling. The Indian Yoga textbook *Gheranda-Samhita*, for example, classifies the prickle feeling as a phenomenon of *bhakti*, devotional love (7, 14-15). And in the Hindu epics and legends, the hair of the bodies of heroes, yogis and gods raise when they behold divine beings or hear timeless truths – like Arjuna, the hero of the *Bhagavadgita*, whose hair stands on end when he recognizes the universal nature of his charioteer, god Krishna (11, 14). And the *Bhagavata Purana*, focused on devotional love for the incarnations of Vishnu, particularly Krishna, clearly states:

"How can without bhakti one's hair stand on end, without loving service the heart melt, without devotion the tears flow, the bliss be and one's consciousness be purified?" (Canto 11, 14, 23).

*Arjuna's hair stand on end as he beholds the true nature of god Krishna. Source: Link[4].*

In religious literature, the prickle feeling is also mentioned as an accompanying aspect of deep contemplation and meditation. In the *Abhidhamma*, the most recent part of the Buddhist Pali canon, the sensation of a prickling indicates a certain level of meditation: after the thoughts have ceased to flow, an overwhelming joy (Pali: *piti*) spreads throughout the whole body which may intensify to total ecstasy. The phenomenon is not unknown to some mystics of the Semitic religions: church father Augustine wrote in the 4th century about a holy shiver that suddenly has come over him and let him recognize the invisible nature of the creation of God. And the 11th century Islamic mystic al-Qusayri connects goose bumps to the state of deep humility (Arabic: *tawadu*) and the disclosure of truth. In addition, the prickle feeling is a phenomenon often reported by members of indigenous societies that frequently use ritual techniques of ecstasy and trances to achieve altered states of consciousness. We have anthropological data suggesting a close connection between goose bumps and ecstatic states or trance from Bengal, Micronesia and South America, where the tingling is often associated with the presence of super-human powers and certain states of the soul.

## Healing through prickling – a holistic and energetic perspective

If the prickle feeling goes together with devotional love, ecstasy and altered states of consciousness in general, we can understand it as a symptom of holistic development and healing. But how does this phenomenon bring about healing?

To answer that question, I suggest thinking of the prickling as a sensation that indicates subtle energy which flows out of the psychosomatic body. This view corresponds with the Ayurvedic teaching that understands the prickling as a sign of an increased *vata dosha* – wind or ethereal – state, and thus as subtle energy. Any prickling with hair standing on end would therefore point to excess energy flowing out of the body on a subtle (*vata*) level. As energy flows out, it dissolves subtle blockades and slags and brings about cooling – just as sweating, urinating and defecating bring about cleaning and cooling on a more material level (*pitta* and *kapha*).

Generally, Western academic medicine does not ascribe cleaning and cooling effects to the prickle phenomenon. Rather, it is known as a symptom of various, often infectious diseases, along with cold, faint, dizziness, numbness and other troubles. There are indications, however, that the prickling is, like fever, a defensive reaction of the body. Fact is that certain medicine can cause prickle feelings in patients. Interpreted from the perspective of energy, the active agent of the medicine causes the patient's subtle energy to flow out of the psychosomatic body through the prickle feeling and, thus, to clear body and mind from the disease. Furthermore, there are statistical studies suggesting "chills", usually accompanied by prickling, to have an unexplored health benefit. It was found that fever patients with blood poisoning who have chills show higher survival rates, compared with those patients who do not experience chills. The researchers suspect that, in general, patients with chills are able to respond more effectively to diseases.

If we proceed to think in line with the energetic-cathartic interpretation, we learn about the cleansing effect of the prickling also on a psychological level. Inner tensions are made conscious and get resolved through the experience of the prickle feeling. In fear situations, for example, it is the energy of fear that we release through our psychosomatic body. With increasing progress, fear symptoms like tremors and heart palpitation will cease to appear. This allows us not only to stay calm and centred in such situations, but we can even learn to enjoy this energy – fear is losing not its energy but its emotional power over us. Likewise, the prickling in the head that is sometimes noticeable in states of intense anger has the effect of a "valve" and allows us to immediately become calm and relaxed. In this way, we have not suppressed the aggression but rather let its energy flow out of our body without being rude or even destructive against ourselves or others – we have overcome the anger. The same happens with strong affection in love or sexuality. A conversation with a sympathetic human being can cause a relaxing prickle feeling – it enables us to enjoy that moment free from possible oppressive constraints and desires. Also, those who try to convert their sexual energy will increasingly experience hair standing on end, indicating the outflow of transformed sexual energy – by way of an ecstatic full body orgasm, which relaxes and strengthens body and mind and lets us experience a beautiful and joyful environment.

*Tibetan Medicine Buddha: Does he heal through his ecstatic energy radiating from his body? Source: Link*[5].

## The prickle feeling from seer Nestor's perspective

In all these cases, the prickle feeling helps us to become aware of emotional tension, to dissolve and release it as pure energy without becoming entrapped in emotional dependencies. Neuropsychological studies indirectly confirmed this when they found that "goose bumps" are associated with increased attention and positive assessments, as well as with reduced anxiety and aversion in the persons examined. Thus, in the sense of a holistic cleansing or development, the prickle feeling has a healing aspect which is inseparable from spirituality. Western medicine and physiology is gradually discovering what was known and exemplified by spiritual masters of different cultures and traditions.

For my mentor, the Emmental seer Nestor, however, there is more to this phenomenon. He interprets this feeling as "pure energy that flow from the body into the pictures as a whole". What does that mean? To Nestor, being human means to constantly take in energy in diverse forms, transform it and release it again as movements on the physical, emotional and intellectual levels. However, for people who want to increase their consciousness intensity, there is a problem with these forms of energy release: physical actions, feelings and thoughts, no matter how ideal and loving they are, always have the disadvantage that they are limiting our consciousness. They go together with certain expectations and intentions, and they are directed to a certain person, a specific situation, a particular object. Thus, they bind us to a reality that we want to overcome. Consciousness development means that, the longer the more, we become able to release energy in a way that is free from such limits – an energetic gift to everyone and everything equally. This form of energy release consists in allowing energy to flow directly from the body to the environment. The feeling that arises in these moments is the ecstatic prickle with the hair standing on end.

At the beginning of our journey, such prickle feelings are rather rare. In addition, we experience the prickle only briefly and not very intense, rather as a tingling accompanied by a shivering and a trembling. Through proper diet, bodily and breathing exercises, meditation and other physical and spiritual practices, we increase our energy metabolism and eliminate internal blockages. If our energy flow increases, prickle feelings are triggered more easily and more often, last longer and flow through the whole body, not just parts of it. In other words: the prickle can be developed in intensity up to that whole-body energy rush that Nestor calls "whole-body orgasm" or "ecstasy" (Greek: *ekstasis*, "stepping outside of oneself"). This also shows the spiritual meaning of ecstasy: it not only frees us of emotions and dependencies, makes us present, relaxed and happy, as the prickle feeling does. It also causes a change of consciousness that manifests, among other things, as a visual change. Nestor reports that ecstasy makes all phenomena in his field of vision appear closer, brighter and sharper, and therefore more intense. This intense bodily bliss is also accompanied by spiritual insights and the feeling of absolute presence.

# References


Augustinus, Aurelius (1838): *Confessiones*, transl. by Georg Rapp. Stuttgart

Becker, Judith O. (2004): *Deep Listeners: Music, Emotion and Trancing*. Info University Press

Figge, Horst H. (1973): *Geisterkult, Besessenheit und Magie in der Umbanda-Religion Brasiliens*. K. Alber

Goodenough, Ward H. (2002): *Under Heaven's Brow: Pre-Christian Religious Tradition in Chuuk*. Philadelphia

Grewe, Oliver et al. (2005): "How Does Music Arouse 'Chills'? Investigating Strong Emotions, Combining Psychological, Physiological, and Psychoacoustical Methods". *Neurosciences and Music III: From Perception to Performance* (Annals of the New York Academy of Sciences 1060): 446-449

Guenther, Herbert V. (1974): *Philosophy and Psychology in the Abhidharma*. Delhi

Hartmann, Richard (1914): *Das Sufitum nach Al-Kuschairi*. J. J. Augustin

McDaniel, June (1989): *The Madness of the Saints. Ecstatic Religion in Bengal*. Chicago

Panksepp, J. (1995): "The emotional sources of 'chills' induced by music". *Music Perception* 13, no. 2: 171-207

Spitzer, Manfred (2002): *Musik im Kopf*. Stuttgart

Tausin, Floco (2009): *Mouches Volantes. Eye Floaters as Shining Structure of Consciousness*. Bern: Leuchtstruktur Verlag

Van Dissel, Jaap T. Et al. (2005): "Chills in 'early sepsis': good for you?" *Journal of Internal Medicine* 257: 469-472

Gieler, Uwe (2002). "Warum bekommt man in besonders bewegenden Momenten eine Gänsehaut?" *Spektrum.de*. spektrum.de/frage/warum-bekommt-man-in-besonders-bewegenden-momenten-eine-gaensehaut/591742 (18.9.22)

# Links

Link[1]: *Ovimagazine.com.* ovimagazine.com/art/7242 (18.9.22)

Link[2]:
photobucket.com/gallery/user/jesse_pindus/media/bWVkaWFJZDo3NDg4OTc
y/?ref= (15.10.19)

Link[3]: trendpickle.com/kamasutra-indian-conception-on-bodily-gratification/
(18.9.22).

Link[4]: pinterest.com/pin/563653709588106174/ (18.9.22)

Link[5]:
photobucket.com/gallery/user/gwandana/media/bWVkaWFJZDo2MjA2NjMy/
?ref= (15.10.19)

# 4

# Eye floaters as a source of inspiration for Carlos Castaneda?

**First published:**

Tausin, Floco (2010): "Cocoons and fibers – Eye floaters as a source of inspiration for Carlos Castaneda?" Source: Link[1].

The anthropologist and cult writer Carlos Castaneda (CC) has substantially contributed to the emergence of a Western New Age shamanism. From the 1960s until his death in April 1998, CC published more than ten books, all of which he declared as anthropologically relevant collections of conversations actually having taken place and experiences made with the Mexican Yaqui Indian and shaman Don Juan Matus (DJ) and his companions. Today, the authenticity of CC's books is strongly controversial far beyond anthropology. But a worldwide total circulation of the order of a million copies testifies that CC's books, critical of society and reason, have been balsam for a whole generation which did not conceal its rejection of bourgeois politics and ideology. The same books were and are still widely received by the generation to follow whose spiritual way to the inside is hardly inspired by religious institutions. They gratefully adopted the fascinating description of a "separate reality", based on experiences of altered consciousness states, supported by the authenticity of Native Indian shamanism, and narrated in a lively dialogic writing style.

Due to my experiences with entoptic (subjective visual) phenomena, I am interested in the visual objects perceived in altered consciousness states described in the books of CC. My question is whether these abstract geometric forms and shapes, as well as the concepts based on them, are inspired by so-called eye floaters (*muscae volitantes* or *mouches volantes*). Eye floaters, transparent dots and strings floating in the visual field in bright light conditions, are thought to be vitreous opacities in ophthalmology. Of course, this interpretation does in no way justice to the spiritual dimension of that phenomenon: according to the teaching of a group of seers from the Swiss Emmental whom I know personally, these dots and strings are first appearances of a whole structure, thought to be created by our consciousness that develops and lightens up as a result of a certain spiritual way of life (Tausin 2009a, 2009b, 2006a, 2006c). I am convinced that, unlike the culturally and individual psychologically conditioned dreams and hallucinations, this consciousness structure is a universal perception that is developed, perceived and interpreted in shamanistic practice since prehistoric times (Tausin 2006b; Lewis-Williams/Dowson 1988). Thus, my thesis is that CC must have known these dots and strings, be it in the everyday or some separate reality, or both.

I follow the somewhat critical interpretation of CC's work, assuming that CC's experience reports are based on altered consciousness states at least partly induced by hallucinogenics; following a good tradition of literary and artistic liberty, he embroidered these experiences and set them into the more or less fictitious context of his apprenticeship with Don Juan (Murray 1979). I'm not going to speculate about facts and fiction, though. Therefore, the initial question cannot be answered with certainty. But understanding CC's experiences in terms of the perception of eye floaters, or entoptics in general, may provide a novel and more realistic understanding of his work which is, to me, a great and impressive account of the human ability to gain knowledge by exploring different modes of perception and extraordinary states of consciousness.

## Subjective visual phenomena

Subjective visual phenomena are not a rarity in Castaneda's books. Moving spots, shades, spherical and string-like shapes and objects are described and worked out continuously.

### 1) Spots and shades

In principle, spots and shades describe those objects which the observer cannot recognize clearly. This applies both to eye floaters which are partly experienced as diffuse spots, shades or dark clouds; and to quick perceptions in CC's books. Again and again,

CC sees shades that are declared by DJ as beings like the death, an ally, or some other supernatural force. *In A Separate Reality*, for example, CC perceives "something like a moth or a spot in my retina" that swept across from right to left between himself and the fire he was looking at; when he looks again, the same shadow glides in the opposite direction. This appearance, reminiscent of the movements of eye floaters, is called a "being" by DJ, and later, significantly, a "bubble" (Castaneda 1971).

Another shade worth mentioning is the so-called "flyer", described only in the tenth book, *The Active Side of Infinity*. The flyer is allegedly a predatory creature that lives on the energy of people's awareness. This "inorganic" being can be perceived as a big shadow, which "leaps through the air" (Castaneda 1997). In an interview published 1995 in the Summer (June-August) issue of *Kindred Spirit* magazine, the three "Chacmool" women Kylie Lundahl, Reni Murez and Nyei Murez declared that "the flyers of the sorcerers' tradition are black shadows that we sometimes detect and explain away as floaters in the retina", making the only explicit link of CC's subjective visual phenomena to eye floaters known to me. However, the description of the flyer hardly applies to floaters: the most obvious difference is the notion that flyers are big impenetrable shades, and that they can be seen only in the dark (Castaneda 1997). Moreover, according to the Carol Tiggs Chronology on the CC legacy website *Sustained Action* (Link [2]), head of Casa Tibet Tony Karam captured a flyer photo which was later displayed by the CC group at several workshops in the 1990s (Donovan 2007). Floaters, on the contrary, are single transparent dots and strands that we see in bright light conditions and which cannot be photographed. Nevertheless, the statement of the Chacmool women shows that the people around CC, and thus highly probable also CC himself, are familiar with the phenomenon of eye floaters.

## 2) The golden bubbles

The bubbles perceived by CC during several altered consciousness states in *A Separate Reality* are described rather obscurely:

> "They were not really bubbles, not like a soap bubble, nor like a balloon, nor any spherical container. They were not containers, yet they were contained. Nor were they round, although when I first perceived them I could have sworn they were round and the image that came to my mind was 'bubbles.' I viewed them as if I were looking through a window; that is, the frame of the window did not allow me to follow them but only permitted me to view them coming into and going out of my field of perception" (Castaneda, 1971).

In the same book, CC experiences their colour as greenish; in *Tales of Power*, he speaks about golden bubbles, referring to the experience cited above. The round shining appearance is also described as a ball or ball of fire in later books (Castaneda 1974, 1984). It is characteristic that these transparent bubbles are strung together and become bigger in the one or the other way: In *A Separate Reality,* CC is advised to follow and mount them, which he eventually succeeds in. In *Tales of Power*, however, the bubbles approach CC and wrap him up. The transparency, the stringing together as well as the getting closer of these bubbles are indications to eye floaters: these dots or spheres, often strung together to strings, are reported and experienced to approach the observer and get bigger in intense consciousness states (Tausin 2009a).

*Transparent bubble. Cover of a German book by Florinda Donner-Grau. Source: Link[3].*

Moreover, these bubbles are visually related to living beings: in a burst (!) bubble, CC sees a friend of him, some other time he sees DJ's friend and seer Genaro appearing out of a bubble (Castaneda 1974). These perceptions match the concept of the bubbles which is drawn up for the first time in *Tales Of Power* in the context of the "explanation of the sorcerers": human beings are living in bubbles which have closed due to our socialization and which must be opened again from inside (by ourselves) or from outside (by the benefactor) in order to recognize the totality of ourselves and attain ultimate freedom. This concept is continuously developed and, speaking of theoretical complexity, reaches its peak in the seventh book, *The Fire from Within*. The concept "bubble" then is gradually replaced by "luminous eggs" or "cocoons", modifying also the notion of the shape: while in the early and middle books we read mainly about circular visual objects, the same objects are described rather longish later.


### 3) Luminous eggs and cocoons


Already in *A Separate Reality*, the form of human beings as it is seen by the seers is described as an "egg of circulating fibers". However, this concept is mentioned only briefly and not further elaborated until the fifth book, *The Second Ring of Power*. Here, the sorceress Gorda explains that only average people look like eggs while sorcerers have the shape of tombstones, round at both ends (Castaneda 1977). In later books, however, there is no insistence on this difference; rather, these visual objects are simply called "eggs" and later "cocoons".

Nevertheless, the descriptions of these eggs or cocoons vary: in the sixth book, *The Eagle's Gift*, CC describes these eggs that "moved in a floating manner" as having an external, darker shell and an inner yellowish shining core (Castaneda 1981). In this and other books, though, we learn that the luminous eggs or cocoons show dark spots, dents or a black hole in their middle, a reference to energy loss which arises from the procreation of children (Castaneda 1977, 1981, 1984). Both descriptions apply to eye floaters: the concentric luminous floater spheres, too, are verifiably of two types, one having a dark shell and a bright core, the other a luminous shell and a dark core.

*Human beings as luminous eggs. Cover of the Italian translation of one of Norbert Classen's book on CC. Source: Link[4].*

Starting with the seventh book, *The Fire From Within,* however, the idea of the luminous and dented cocoons takes on such a complexity that the comparison with eye floaters is difficult again: the cocoons consist of a variety of fibres (see below) and do not simply enclose a core but a bundle of bands, called the "Eagle's emanations". Next to the spots, holes or dents already mentioned, there is a gap in this cocoon. After DJ, death, as a "rolling force", would come through this gap and break open the cocoon. This force is also called "tumbler" and is described as approaching balls of fire (Castaneda 1984) – which, in turn, could be another vision inspired by the perception of eye floaters in intense consciousness states. DJ explains that this cocoon shows a bright spot or point in the upper area and on the surface, the "assemblage point", mentioned and elaborated only from the seventh book on. This point groups a number of emanation bands while shifting within the bounds of these emanations, causing and determining man's perception of the world. Due to our integration into society it is fixed but can be released by appropriate practices and shifted inside the cocoon to allow the perception of completely different worlds (Castaneda 1984).

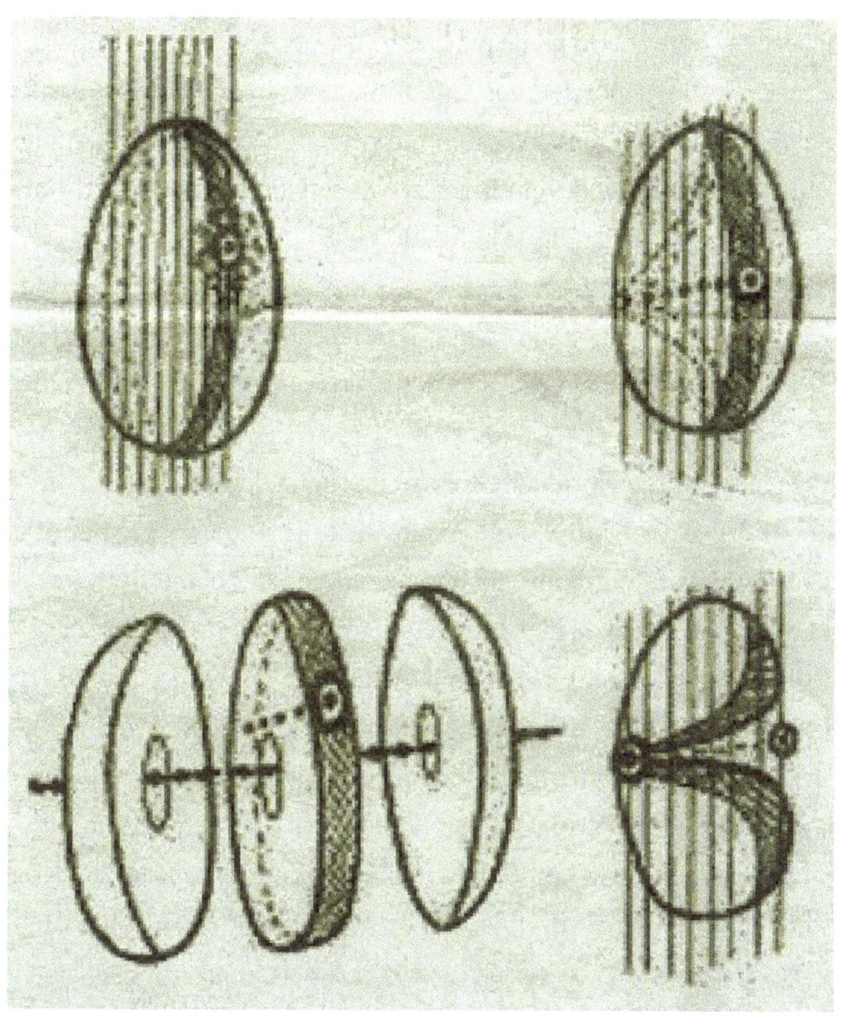

*Cocoon with assemblage point. Source: Link[5].*

How could the assemblage point be related to eye floaters? One could describe that point as a brighter core on or in a darker cocoon – that is one of the two kinds of eye floater spheres. Plus, there is a corresponding and rare perception of floater spheres in states of deep concentration (of the observer and the sphere) where the core seems to be pushed to the periphery of the sphere. However, the elaborated concept of the assemblage point with its qualities and functions in relation to perception and manipulation can hardly be brought into harmony with the luminous spheres of eye floaters (Tausin 2009a, 2006c).


## *4) The lines of the world*

The "lines of the world" are for the first time discussed in the third book, *Journey to Ixtlan*. DJ explains that these lines come out of various parts of our body; the most durable lines come from the middle of the body. They connect us with the world, and one can feel them. "Not-doing" is the practice to feel the world through these lines. A little later, CC perceives the lines while looking into the sun over the horizon. In principle, the "lines of the world" could point to the strings of eye floaters that are seen best and become luminous in bright light conditions and in a concentrated state of mind. However, it is said one can act upon someone using these lines, and in *Tales of Power*, the descriptions of physical shifting by means of these lines  start (Castaneda 1972, 1974). Moreover, the term of the "lines", like that of the "bubble", is not constant: in later books, it is replaced by the terms "filaments", "strings" and "fibers".

## 5) *Filaments, strings, fibers, and tentacles*

The perception of filaments, strings and fibres is a continuous topic with CC. These filaments are described as being luminous and vibrating. In most cases, the fibres are connected with the perception of a human being as a luminous egg or cocoon: the luminous egg of man consists of these fibres, and the fibres come out of the middle of the body or the egg, respectively. On the other hand, these fibres may appear independently of the perception of the luminous balls or eggs, for example in *Journey to Ixtlan* where CC views a mountain range as an array of light fibres, or when CC is told that the whole cosmos consists of these fibres and that we are connected to everything by them (Castaneda 1972).

"Filament" and "string" are used equivalently; so is "fiber" and "filament"/"strings", until the relationship between the two is clarified and the concepts expanded in *The Eagle's Gift* and *The Fire from Within*. Here, a string is a thin fibre while a thick fibre is described as a "tentacle". As is the case with "lines", sorcerers are thought to gain information about a person or to manipulate or cure a person by leaving their fibres in him or her during interaction. Also, these fibres serve for the paranormal shifting: by means of them, a sorcerer can grip anything in the area and drag himself to that spot; doing this, he or she overcomes gravity and is able to fly physically. The reference to the eye floater strings is vague, because, on the one hand, they are described merely as shining and vibrating, and, on the other hand, because of their fanciful shifting function that goes far beyond the bare seeing.

## *6) The bands of emanations*

In *The Fire from Within*, finally, DJ introduces the "great bands of emanations", a visual experience that integrates all of the main visual objects so far: these bands of emanations are understood as the clusters of the emanations of the Eagle, the power that governs the destiny of all living beings. There are 48 of these bands, but only one is said to produce organic beings:

"For instance, there is an immeasurable cluster that produces organic beings. The emanations of that organic band have a sort of fluffiness. They are transparent and have a unique light of their own, a peculiar energy. They are aware, they jump. That's the reason why all organic beings are filled with a peculiar consuming energy. The other bands are darker, less fluffy. Some of them have no light at all, but a quality of opaqueness. … Think of it as an enormously wide band of luminous filaments, luminous strings with no end. Organic beings are bubbles that grow around a group of luminous filaments" (Castaneda 1984).

*Band of Emanations? Painting by Mars-1 (Mario Martinez), exhibited at White Walls (Tenderloin, SF), showing "Mescalito" in 2006. Source: Link[6].*

This visual experience of the seers has much in common with the perception of eye floaters in intense consciousness states: floaters are seen to belong to several layers; strings and spheres (bubbles) look transparent or luminous, blurred or focused, dependent on the ability of concentration; spheres are inside or around the strings; they don't float anymore but jump (viz. the consciousness light illuminates different strings and bubbles) (Tausin 2009a, 2006c).

## Conclusions

In CC's books, there is no explicit indication that the extraordinary perceptions of subjective visual phenomena are, in fact, eye floaters. However, we find a partial correspondence of CC's descriptions of such phenomena with the reports of the Swiss seers of the Emmental on the visual experience of eye floaters in various states of consciousness, my own visual experience included (Tausin 2009a, 2006c). The bubbles, the balls of fire, the luminous eggs and the cocoons can absolutely be understood as the luminous dots or spheres of floaters, while the energy lines, filaments, fibres and tentacles point to the luminous floater strings. However, the comparison of CC's visual phenomena with eye floaters is made difficult by the fact that the meanings and descriptions of the phenomena mentioned are not constant but change through the books of CC: the appearance and function of the round and string-like objects  become increasingly complex and detailed.

In my opinion, it is nevertheless not only possible but very likely that CC knew the phenomenon of eye floaters, and that they had an inspiring effect on his work, for two reasons: first, eye floaters are known to the people around CC, as was shown in the interview of the Chacmool women. Second, it is hardly conceivable to me that someone who enters intensive consciousness states for many years to explore very attentively the most subtle visual phenomena never gets a glimpse of these dots and strings of eye floaters. The connection of consciousness and eye floaters may not be recognized in the beginning; but over the years and after careful examinations of the visual phenomena in relation to the extraordinary consciousness states, the observer will, in my opinion, recognize the deeper meaning of eye floaters.

Whether CC was that observer is, in turn, another question. And that brings us to the crucial question: if CC's work is actually inspired by eye floaters, as I assume, why don't we find that clearly stated in any of his books? The following scenarios are conceivable:

**1)** CC couldn't see eye floaters and knew nothing about them. In this case it would have been DJ (or whoever was his informant and teacher) who reported about his extraordinary visual perceptions of luminous balls and strings – and perhaps embroidered these reports himself. If that person was actually a Mexican Indian without access to Western academic knowledge, it can be assumed that he did not know about the ophthalmologic explanation of eye floaters.

**2)** CC couldn't see eye floaters but he let himself be inspired by pre-Columbian Native American art. This art often consists of geometric ornamentations (e.g. spheres and strings) and in many cases is a depiction of entoptic phenomena (e.g. eye floaters) perceived by shamans during their visionary experiences (Tausin 2006b, 2007a; Thurston 1991). In both of these cases, modern medical explanations and studies on entoptic phenomena and shamanistic art, starting in the late 1980s, would have never been subject of the conversations between CC and DJ.

**3)** CC has seen the eye floaters and maybe even recognized their deeper meaning due to his consciousness altering practices. In his books, however, he transfigured his perceptions very strongly, referring to Native American shamanistic mythology. Perhaps CC even knew the medical explanation of that entoptic phenomenon from the beginning. However, there was no point in providing that medical or ophthalmological approach in his books, for, on the one hand, his audience was looking for the fantastic and spiritual aspects of reality, not the academic ones; and on the other hand, his work would have become a pathological dimension in a time when many anthropologists were still doubting the sanity of shamans in general.

Anyway: CC's work not only demands a great deal of tolerance and imagination by its elaborated descriptions of altered states of consciousness, but also opens up a big range of interpretation by its theoretical and conceptual expansions and complexity – an interpretation range in which eye floaters fit with a high degree of probability. Symptomatic for this is a particular situation in *The Fire From Within* where DJ interprets CC's perception of the balls of fire in more detail: out of these balls of fire, he said, there "comes an iridescent hoop exactly the size of living beings, whether men, trees, microbes or allies". When CC asks about the possibility of different-sized circles, DJ protests: "Don't take me so literally."

# References

Castaneda, Carlos (1968): *The Teachings of Don Juan. A Yaqui Way of Knowledge.* University of California Press

Castaneda, Carlos (1971): *A Separate Reality. Further Conversations with Don Juan.* New York: Simon & Schuster

Castaneda, Carlos (1972): *Journey to Ixtlan. The Lessons of Don Juan.* New York: Simon & Schuster

Castaneda, Carlos (1974): *Tales of Power.* New York: Simon & Schuster

Castaneda, Carlos (1977): *The Second Ring of Power.* New York: Simon & Schuster

Castaneda, Carlos (1981): *The Eagle's Gift.* New York: Simon & Schuster

Castaneda, Carlos (1984): *The Fire From Within.* New York: Simon & Schuster

Castaneda, Carlos (1987): *The Power of Silence. Further Lessons of Don Juan.* New York: Simon & Schuster

Castaneda, Carlos (1993): *The Art of Dreaming.* New York: Haper Collins

Castaneda, Carlos (1997): *The Active Side of Infinity.* New York: Harper Collins

Donovan, Corey (2007): "Carol Tiggs. Chronolog Part IV (1994-May 1995)". *Sustainedaction.org.* sustainedaction.org/Chronologies/chronTiggsIV.htm (19.9.22)

Lewis-Williams, J. D.; Dowson, T. A. (1988): "The Signs of All Times: Entoptic Phenomena in Upper Paleolithic Art". *Current Anthropology* 29, no. 2: 201-245

Murray, Stephen O. (1979): "The Scientific Reception of Castaneda". *Contemporary Sociology* 8, no. 2: 189-192

Tausin, Floco (2009a): *Mouches Volantes. Eye Floaters as Shining Structure of Consciousness.* Bern: Leuchtstruktur Verlag

Tausin, Floco (2009b): "Open Eye Meditation. The visual way to the development of the inner sense". *The International Journal of Healing and Caring (IJHC)* 9, no. 3. wholistichealingresearch.com/ijhchome (28.8.09)

Tausin, Floco (2007a): "Entoptic Art – Entoptische Erscheinungen als Inspirationsquelle in der zeitgenössischen bildenden Kunst". *Extremnews.com.* extremnews.com/berichte/vermischtes/396b116f79905e4 (19.9.22)

Tausin, Floco (2006a): "Zwischen Innenwelt und Aussenwelt. Entoptische Phänomene und ihre Bedeutung für Bewusstseinsentwicklung und Spiritualität". *Schlangentanz* 3

Tausin, Floco (2006b): "Mouches volantes und Trance. Ein universelles Phänomen bei erweiterten Bewusstseinszuständen früher und heute". *Jenseits des Irdischen* 3

Tausin, Floco (2006c): "Mouches volantes. Bewegliche Kugeln und Fäden aus der Sicht eines Sehers". *Q'Phaze. Realität ... Anders!* 4

Thurston, Linda (1991): *Entoptic Imagery in People and Their Art* (M.A. thesis, 1991, web edition 1997). home.comcast.net/~markk2000/thurston/thesis.html (2011)

n/a. (1995): "A New Generation Of Sorcerers. Kindred Spirit 1". *Oldnagualnet.com.* oldnagualnet.com/wtg/INTERVIEWS/KINDRED1.HTML (2010)

## Links

Link[1]: *New-age-spirituality.com.* new-age-spirituality.com/wordpress/content/884 (19.9.22)

Link[2]: sustainedaction.org (19.9.22)

Link[3]: castaneda.witchpage.de (2010)

Link[4]: carloscastaneda.it/Libri-Castaneda/Norbert-Classen-Carlos-Castaneda-e-i-Guerrieri-di-don-Juan.htm (19.9.22)

Link[5]: carloscastaneda.it/Visione-Tolteca.htm (19.9.22)

Link[6]: fecalface.com/SF/index.php?option=com_content&task=view&id=367&Itemid=90 (19.9.22)

# 5

# Eye Floaters and Near-Death Experiences

**First published:**

Tausin, Floco (2012): "The Shining Sphere at the End of the Tunnel". Source: Link[1].

Stories of individuals near to their death are known from many cultures and times. For Western people of past centuries, near-death phenomena attested to the existence of heaven and hell. At the end of the 19th century, such experiences became the focal point of individual scientists' research. But it was only in the second half of the 20th century that this phenomenon came across a wider scientific and public interest. After preliminary work by researchers such as Elisabeth Kübler-Ross, Russell Noyes and Robert Crookall (cp. Corazza 2008), the philosopher and psychiatrist Raymond Moody published his book *Life after life* in 1975. It became a best-seller and initiated the popularization of the subjects of death and dying which were strongly tabooed in Western societies at that time. People from all social classes were encouraged to share their encounters with death. This development has led to a steady increase of near-death experience (NDE) reports in the past thirty years.

According to different surveys (cp. Schick/Vaughn 2010), 18 to 60 percent of the patients having suffered a severe accident or cardiac arrest experience sensory and cognitive impressions during their "clinical death" – impressions that Moody collectively calls "near-death experiences". In the literature, this term is sometimes confined against the "deathbed visions" that are experienced by sick and infirm people in the final stage of the dying process. Moody, after having compared dozens of near-death accounts, describes several elements that NDEs typically consist of:

"A man is dying and, as he reaches the point of greatest physical distress, he hears himself pronounced dead by his doctor. He begins to hear an uncomfortable noise, a loud ringing or buzzing, and at the same time feels himself moving very rapidly through a long dark tunnel. After this, he suddenly finds himself outside of his own physical body, but still in the immediate physical environment, and he sees his own body from a distance, as though he is a spectator. He watches the resuscitation attempt from this unusual vantage point and is in a state of emotional upheaval. After a while, he collects himself and becomes more accustomed to his odd condition. He notices that he still has a 'body,' but one of a very different nature and with very different powers from the physical body he has left behind. Soon other things begin to happen. Others come to meet and to help him. He glimpses the spirits of relatives and friends who have already died, and a loving, warm spirit of a kind he has never encountered before – a being of light – appears before him. This being asks him a question, nonverbally, to make him evaluate his life and helps him along by showing him a panoramic, instantaneous playback

of the major events of his life. At some point he finds himself approaching some sort of barrier or border, apparently representing the limit
between earthly life and the next life. Yet, he finds that he must go back
to the earth, that the time for his death has not yet come. At this point he
resists, for by now he is taken up with his experiences in the afterlife
and does not want to return. He is overwhelmed by intense feelings of
joy, love, and peace. Despite his attitude, though, he somehow reunites
with his physical body and lives" (Moody 1975).

This model account – based on a catalogue of recurring elements
– was soon challenged by other researchers who extended or
shortened it (cp. Knoblauch 1999). This fact shows that NDEs are
by no means identical, but contain both similarities and differences regarding their content and sequence of elements.

Individuals experience their state of near-death as real and pro-
found. Following an NDE, they often change their views, beliefs
and values regarding their environment, fellow human beings,
death and the hereafter. They often begin to strive for a more loving and more social way of life than before. In some people,
NDEs seem to have enhanced intellectual or psychical abilities or
have spontaneously cured diseases. Even some religious or spiritual movements are inspired by the experience of near-death.
Negative after-effects are less frequently reported, e.g. the frustra-
tion of being confronted with everyday challenges again, or the
feelings of loneliness due to the difficulties in sharing the experience with, and being understood by, related parties. And in the
case of negative NDEs, individuals' fear of dying may increase
(Corazza 2008; Greyson 2006; Horacek 1997).

**Explanations**

The term "near-death" is unspecific insofar as it includes several elements that are found not only in NDEs but also in other altered states of consciousness. Near-death-like phenomena may be triggered by extreme fatigue, shamanic or meditation practices, centrifuge training for pilots (G-LOC syndrome), prolonged social isolation, sensory deprivation, dreams, mind-altering plants and substances (NDEs are reported to be induced by ketamine and dimethyltryptamine, DMT). In the literature, the similarities or differences between these experiences and the NDEs are highlighted, accepted or rejected, according to the author's position (Corazza 2008; Strassman 2006; Grof/Halifax 1977; Moody 1975). Accordingly, several hypotheses about the nature and meaning of NDEs circulate today; none of them could be proven or rejected so far:

### 1) *The biological theory*

According to this materialistic theory, there is no consciousness or soul that could exist without the physical body. Elements of NDEs, therefore, are understood as different physiological processes in the moments of physical death: lack of oxygen and the collapse of inhibitory mechanisms in the brain (over)stimulate the neuronal activity of the visual system and lead to the perception of light and tunnel-like shapes; stimulation of the limbic system and the release of neurotransmitters like endorphins are responsible for experiences of analgesia, peace, love and euphoria; out-of-body experiences (OBE), life reviews and the perception of other-worldly landscapes are the results of the stimulation of the brain's temporal lobe, neurologically releasing memories and inducing hallucinations and processes of depersonalization. Sceptics further emphasize that the study of NDEs does not provide insights about death and possible forms of existence hereafter, because the temporary "clinical death" is not to be equated with final death (irreversible tissue death) (cp. n/a 2009; Blackmore 1993, 2005; Blackmore/Troscianko 1988).


## *2) The cultural historical explanation*

Descriptions or investigations of the phenomenon of NDE often imply universalistic assumptions. Most prominent is the idea that all NDEs contain the same or similar elements or perceptions in the same or similar sequence. While biologists contribute to that idea by asserting the universal functioning of the brain, religiously or spiritually inspired individuals recognize similarities in NDEs across all cultures in order to confirm the universal truth of their respective versions of the hereafter.

Still, near-death researchers do not agree about which elements of NDEs are to be viewed as central or even universal. For the contents of NDE reports vary significantly, depending on time and place. For example, elements like OBE, movement in a tunnel and life review are typical for modern Western NDEs, but are negligible in reports about near-death states from the past or other cultures (Knoblauch 1999; Kellehear 1996). But cultural scientists also establish similarities in NDEs: in many past and present cultures, individuals in states of near-death are likely to shift to other realms where they meet deceased relatives or supernatural beings. These other worlds have great similarities with the architecture, fashion and social structure of the individuals' everyday environment. Also, the religious entities that often appear in NDEs are known from the respective culture. This suggests, on the one hand, that NDEs are not independent from cultural specifics, while on the other hand, NDEs may have inspired traditional concepts of the afterlife. NDEs, thanatology, and the history of religion or culture seem to interact in a web of mutual influence (Shushan 2009; Corazza 2008; Athappilly et al. 2006; Knoblauch 1999; Kellehear 1996).


## 3) *The survival theory*

Both biological-reductionist and cultural history approaches negate or ignore the question about the continued existence of consciousness after physical death. For most people with a NDE, however, there is no doubt: They have directly experienced that death is not the end of their existence. They are supported by researchers such as Elisabeth Kübler-Ross, Raymond Moody, Kenneth Ring and others that understand NDEs as a strong indication – if not evidence – for the existence of human consciousness (spirit, soul) without the physical body (cp. Williams Cook et al.

1998). The survival theory is not tied to any specific religious or spiritual tradition. Even though NDEs may contain culturally shaped imagery, people concerned often are surprised that the experience did not meet their religious expectations (Moody 1975, cp. Corazza 2008). Still, individuals tend to interpret their NDE in terms of their religious background. Therefore, Christian believers often find evidence of heaven and hell in their NDE; perception of intense light is often associated with God, Jesus or even – as some Christian critics suggest – with "Lucifer" (from Latin, "the bringer of light") (Rawlings 1987; cp. Knoblauch 1999).

*Dante and Beatrice gaze upon the Empyrean, the highest heaven. A NDE inspirated – or inspiring – scene from the Divine Comedy by Dante Alighieri, illustrated by Gustave Doré. Source: Link[2].*

## 4) *The mystical or spiritual theory*

Even without assuming a mind-body dualism and the survival theory, NDEs can be interpreted as spiritually relevant experiences. Elements like the experience of peace, love and feeling safe, the ineffability of the experience, the presence of a superhuman entity, the transcendence of time and space, and the perception of a bright light or being of light – such aspects are similar to the descriptions of God experiences by visionary mystics of many cultures. One obvious difference is, of course, that near-death experiencers usually did not look for mystical experiences (Grof/Halifax 1977; Zaleski 1993; Cressy 1994; Greyson 2006).

## The ecstatic-entoptic theory

The ecstatic-entoptic view that I suggest is a variation of the mystical  or spiritual theory, but also includes  aspects of the other above mentioned explanatory approaches. It is based on the mystical teachings of an Emmental seer, Nestor, with whom I stayed and learned for many years (cp. Tausin 2009).

## *Ecstasy and the "navel"*

To understand the ecstatic-entoptic interpretation of NDEs, we first have to know the role of ecstasy and entoptic phenomena in the teachings of Nestor. According to him, human beings construct their own world by transforming energy into the concrete natural and cultural phenomena we know from our everyday lives. The flow and outcome of that transformation is shaped by our – psychologically and culturally influenced – state of consciousness. Through a certain style of life and practices, we can increase the flow of energy and free ourselves from bindings to worldly phenomena. As a consequence, the release of energy becomes increased and more direct by way of the prickle feelings of ecstasy. This, in turn, alters our cognition and perception. For example, abstract light phenomena will intensify and occur more frequently in our subjective field of vision. Nestor and his seer-friends report about a network of luminous spheres and strings that they call the "shining structure of consciousness". In an early stage of seeing and consciousness developing, these spheres and strings may be perceived as so-called "eye floaters" or "entoptic phenomena" (cp. Tausin 2012a). By releasing ecstatic energy through ecstasy, our consciousness moves forward in this shining structure. On this journey, we will reach our individual "navel" – a unique sphere to which we are attached. The Emmental seers assert that our consciousness involuntary approaches and even enters the navel in states of intense consciousness and deep relaxation, as well as when falling asleep and when dying. Approaching the navel during lifetime is the goal of the mystic path in the shining structure (Tausin 2011a, 2010a, 2010b, 2009).

Thus, in terms of the ecstatic-entoptic view, dying means releasing all life energy from the body. In Western ancient and biblical tradition, this is called the pneuma or spiritus, breath or soul-as-breath, which leaves the body. In terms of physiology, this release is reflected by a massive random firing of neurons (cp. n/a 2009). In that process, visual perception changes significantly and may be roughly differentiated into two phases: in a first phase, individuals will see abstract light phenomena, e.g. moving in a structure of shining spheres and strings, or moving through a series of spheres or through a dark tunnel towards a shining sphere. In a second phase, when the release of energy decreases, these abstract light phenomena will turn into figurative images which are shaped by the culture and the living environment of the individual. This corresponds to the end of the flight of an individual consciousness, falling into a dream state and trying to construct a stable world again. These two phases – a first abstract or light phase which gradually merges into a second, figurative phase – are especially known from cultures with shamanic traditions and experimental studies with hallucinogens (e.g. Reichel-Dolmatoff 1975, 1978; Lewis-Williams/Dowson 1988; cp. Tausin 2012b). *The Tibetan Book of the Dead* (*Bardo Thodol*) for example, influenced by the shamanic Bon tradition, states that the deceased will perceive the 'clear light' in the first bardo or intermediate state, then tends to experience figurative scenes; the text is read to the deceased in order to guide him through different illusory figurative images and encourage him to follow the clear light (Rinpoche 1996). A contemporary Western example of that two-phase psychedelic trip would be the final sequence of Stanley Kubrick's *2001: A Space Odyssey*: Astronaut Dave Bowman flies through a star gate and experiences a stream of abstract and coloured lights, slowly merging into landscapes  and eventually into a full furnished cosmic hotel room, where he sees himself dying and being reborn.

The duration and intensity of the abstract phase depends on the individual consciousness: generally, it is prolonged and more intense in energetic, open-minded and conscious individuals, whereas people less energetic and conscious will experience their (final) ecstasy rather as a series of figurative images. This general process does not exclude cases of abruptly changing consciousness states. This is suggested by NDE reports in which the sequence is reversed or figurative and abstract images alternate, e.g. the emergence of a redemptive light during "hell visions" (cp. Rawlings 1987), or, according to the *Tibetan Book of the Dead*, the soul's general ability to realize the clear light even in the bardos which feature figurative images and visions.

### Shining Structure Floaters in NDEs?

Thus, the ecstatic-entoptic theory suggests that the abstract contents of visual perception in NDEs correspond to seeing entoptic phenomena in altered states of consciousness. To support the thesis, we will have a closer look at that content and its similarities to one particular type of entoptics, the shining structure floaters.

*Abstract forms – spheres and tubes*

The typical structures of floaters occur in several NDE elements. For example, there are descriptions of tubular or thread-like structures. Rawlings, for example, describes the experience of a man in the following words:

"Moving at high speed through a net of great luminosity, he described going through what appeared to be a grid of luminous strands. After he stopped, this vibrant luminosity became blinding in intensity and drained him of energy. There was no pain and no unpleasant sensation. The grid had transformed him into a form beyond time and space" (Rawlings 1991).

Another element is the psychic "umbilical cord", noted by Robert Crookall, a British pioneer in the clinical study of NDEs. Experiencers repeatedly report about an elastic "cord" or "thread" that appears between them and their physical body. In his interpretation, Crookall draws attention to similar phenomena in the Tibetan culture – a "strand" subsisting between the soul body and the physical body – and to the "silver cord" mentioned in Ecclesiastes 12:5-7. According to him, this cord connects the individual consciousness or soul with the physical body (cp. Steiger/Steiger 2003; n/a 2010a). Again another and frequently mentioned element is moving through a tubular structure that might correspond to the "shining structure" of consciousness. According to the ecstatic-entoptic thesis, it is reasonable to assume a continuity between the abstract and the rather figurative forms of this tubular structure: Depending on the individual level or state of consciousness, the soul's movement through the shining structure may be experienced in a rather abstract (tube, tunnel) or figurative (path, river etc.) way (cp. Shushan 2009; Athappilly et al. 2006; Knoblauch 1999; Kellehear 1996). I therefore assume that the tunnel experience is a central NDE element throughout history and culture. In any case, the famous painting *Ascent of the Blessed* by Dutch artist Hieronymus Bosch (ca. 1450-1516) proves that the tunnel experience is known for centuries.

*Ascent of the Blessed (1500-1504), by Hieronymus Bosch, oil on wood, 87 x 40 cm. Source: Link[3].*

The tunnel in this image shows some details which lead to considering the other floater shape, the sphere: Bosch's tunnel seems to be divided into several segments. This corresponds to the many NDE reports in which the segments or walls of the tunnel are experienced as spheres (e.g. "spherical", "round" etc.). One of Moodys interviewees said that after a feeling of peace and quiet, she found herself "in a tunnel – a tunnel of concentric circles" (Moody 1975). Similarly, German singer and near-death experiencer Anke Hachfeld (Mila Mar, MiLù) describes this tunnel as "illuminated by bright light, spatially limited by soft, round, foam-like forms"; she composes: "I have flown through coloured soft spheres" (Anke n/a).

*Reaching the shining sphere at the end of the tunnel. Source: Link[4].*

Even outside this tube or tunnel, (concentric) spheres or rows of spheres are mentioned in NDEs. This is supported by the investigation of the relationship between NDEs and so-called orbs. Orbs are transparent luminous spheres on photographs that are often interpreted as the souls of the dead (cp. McFetridge 2008; Williams 2007; Tausin 2007, 2008). Fact is that luminous and coloured spheres are frequently witnessed in NDEs, sometimes along with the perception of figurative images like buildings or human-like beings. Also, the beings of light are often experienced as luminous and mobile spheres which sometimes change their shape to anthropomorphic figures. Some experiencers even report about "millions of spheres of light" (Williams 2007).

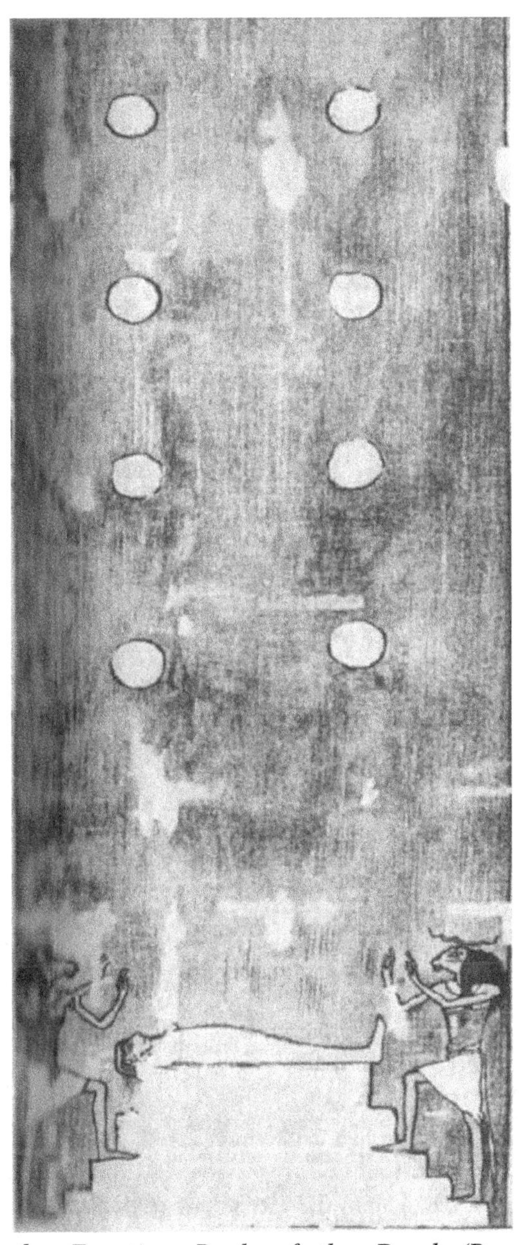

*Scene from the Egyptian Book of the Dead (Papyrus Anhai): The mummy lies on the topmost step of the heavenly stairway and observes the "depths of space", symbolized by eight white disks on a blue ground – shining spheres in the afterlife? Source: Champdor 1977.*

The sphere is not only associated with the tunnel and the being of light, but also with the experiencers' body: During a NDE, individuals realize that they have a new body with expanded capabilities of cognition, perception and movement. This body may be shaped as both, a human being or a sphere – it also may transform from one into the other. Some near-death experiencers also feel themselves enveloped in a sphere (cp. Williams 2007; Rawlings 1987; Moody 1975).


*Light and Darkness*

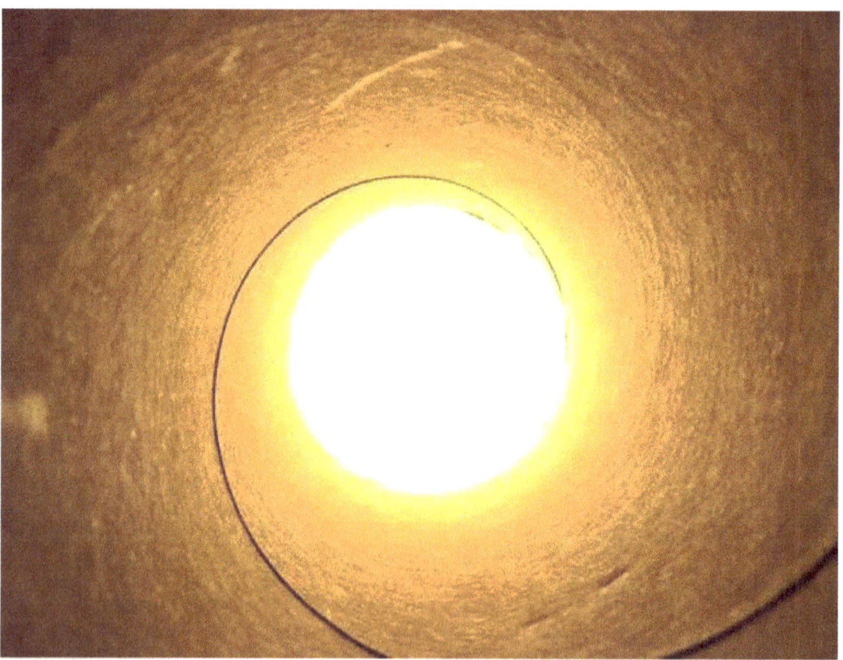

*Light in the darkness. Source: Link[5].*

Light and darkness are also key elements that are mentioned in both modern NDE and ancient beliefs about the afterlife (Shushan 2009). Often, the perception or sensation of darkness is associated with the fall of the soul and the underworld or hell. In contrast, light symbolizes the ascent of the soul and the heavenly abodes. Light and darkness seem to be separated, but both may occur in the same visual scene. For example, a light may appear in the darkness, often described as a clear white light that intensifies when the individual approach it. Also, the light may be accompanied by figurative and concrete imagery – some experiencers personalize the light as a divine being and remember having had a kind of mental conversation with this light. Similar processes are observed with floaters: Both light and darkness are part of the shining structure, as the core-surround principle divides the structure into light and dark areas. Therefore, floaters may be experienced as dark, as opacities (of the vitreous). But as stated above, the more ecstatic energy is given into this structure – depending on the intensity of the consciousness – the more luminous it becomes. It is possible that these energy-related perceptions of light and darkness continue in NDEs.


*The motion (zoom effect, jumps)*


In intense states of consciousness and moments of ecstasy, "zoom effects" may occur in the visual perception (Tausin 2010a): A perceived object lights up and "zooms in" rather abruptly. The Emmental seers understand that phenomenon as the forward movement of the consciousness in the shining structure, towards the navel. In NDEs, when consciousness leaves the physical body, "zoom effects" are experienced frequently, e.g. when flowing or flying through the tunnel or through a dark area towards a bright light. Sometimes, individuals experience this effect in an earlier stage, when still seeing earthly things (cp. Moody 1975). Others see or feel spheres approaching to them (Jinny 2010). Beings of light, often in the form of spheres, also are experienced as highly mobile, "bouncing" or "swirling" (Williams 2007). These examples indicate continuity from the advanced seeing of shining structure floaters to the luminous spheres appearing in NDEs.

## Conclusion

The abstract elements of NDEs have many parallels to entoptic phenomena. It is therefore possible that phenomena like shining structure floaters are perceived in states of near-death. If entoptic phenomena are understood in terms of physiology, NDEs would indeed have a biological or physiological dimension (cp. Tausin 2011b). It would be wrong, however, to reduce NDEs to physiology. We do not know for sure whether physiological processes are the cause or the effect of consciousness, or whether we better understand them as just another level of expression of consciousness. Correspondingly, it is possible that the perception of so-called entoptic phenomena continues even without the physical body. Altered states of consciousness like dreams, mystical rapture and – as pointed out in this article – NDEs suggest that shining structure floaters are a consciousness phenomenon which can be experienced with another, more subtle body. If so, then we experience some kind of NDE when observing or meditating on shining structure floaters. In other words: in focusing on floaters and investigating their nature, we are dealing with something that seems to persist not only in life, but beyond.

# References

n/a (2010a): "Does a Mind Need a Brain?" *The Epoch Times,* 23.6.2010. theepochtimes.com/n2/content/view/37907/ (19.1.11)

n/a (2010b): "Nahtoderfahrungs-Studie: Erste Ergebnisse im kommenden Jahr". *Grenzwissenschaft-Aktuell,* 28.10.2010. grenzwissenschaft-aktuell.blogspot.com/2010/10/nahtoderfahrungs-studie-erste.html (19.9.22)

n/a (2009): "Studie: Gehirnaktivität steigt kurz vor dem Tod stark an". *Grenzwissenschaft-Aktuell,* 8.10.2009. grenzwissenschaft-aktuell.blogspot.com/2009/10/studie-gehirnaktivitat-steigt-kurz-vor.html (19.9.22)

Athappilly, Geena K. et al. (2006). "Do Prevailing Societal Models Influence Reports of Near-Death Experiences? A Comparison of Accounts Reported Before and After 1975". *The Journal of Nervous and Mental Disease* 194, no. 3: 218-222

Blackmore, Susan J. (1993): *Dying to Live: Near-Death Experiences.* Buffalo: Prometheus Books

Blackmore, Susan (2005). *Consciousness. A Very Short Introduction.* Oxford/New York: Oxford University Press

Champdor, Albert (1977): *Das Ägyptische Totenbuch. Kult und Religion im alten Ägypten – nach den schönsten Papyri aus berühmten Grabmälern, aufgefunden in der Nekropole von Theben.* Bern/München: Scherz Verlag

Greyson, Bruce (2006): "Near-Death Experiences and Spirituality". *Zygon* 41, no. 2: 393-414

Grof, Stanislav; Halifax, Joan (1977): *The Human Encounter With Death.* New York: E. P. Dutton

Hachfeld, Anke. (n/a) "Nahtoderfahrung – Ein persönlicher Erlebnisbericht, Informationen und Leseanregungen". *Milamar.de.* milamar.de/flash_site/Nahtoderfahrung2.pdf (19.9.22)

Horacek, Bruce J. (1997): "Amazing Grace: The Healing Effects of Near-Death Experiences on Those Dying and Grieving". *Journal of Near-Death Studies* 16, no. 2: 149-161

Jinny (2010): "Dem Tod ganz nah – Nahtod-Erfahrungen von saira84" (commentary to the article). *Os-community.de.*

www14.os-community.de/Magazin/Dem_Tod_ganz_nah_Nahtod-Erfahrungen/22651 (17.1.11)

Kellehear, Allan (1996): *Experiences Near Death: Beyond Medicine and Religion*. Oxford University Press

Knoblauch, Hubert (1999). *Berichte aus dem Jenseits. Mythos und Realität der Nahtod-Erfahrung*. Freiburg/Basel/Wien: Herder

Lewis-Williams, J. D.; Dowson, T. A. (1988): "The Signs of All Times: Entoptic Phenomena in Upper Paleolithic Art". *Current Anthropology* 29, no. 2: 201-245

McFetridge, Grant (2008): "OBE konzentrische Kugeln" (Glossar des Instituts für das Studium von Peak States). *Peakstates.at.* peakstates.at/glossar.html#no (19.9.22)

Moody, Raymond (2002): *Leben nach dem Tod: die Erforschung einer unerklärlichen Erfahrung* (34. Aufl.). Reinbek bei Hamburg: Rowohlt

Rätsch, Christian (2004): *Enzyklopädie der psychoaktiven Pflanzen. Botanik, Ethnopharmakologie und Anwendungen*. AT Verlag

Rawlings, Maurice S. (1991): *Beyond Death's Door*. Bantam

Reichel-Dolmatoff, Gerardo (1975): *The Shaman and the Jaguar. A Study of Narcotic Drugs Among the Indians of Colombia*. Philadelphia: Temple University Press

Reichel-Dolmatoff, Gerardo (1978): *Beyond the Milky Way. Hallucinatory Imagery of the Tukano Indians*. Los Angeles: University of California

Rinpoche, Sogyal (1996): *Das tibetische Buch vom Leben und Sterben. Ein Schlüssel zum tieferen Verständnis von Leben und Tod* (18. Aufl.). BARTH O. W. Verlag

Schick, Theodore; Vaughn, Lewis (2010): *How to Think About Weird Things: Critical Thinking for a New Age*. (6. Aufl.) McGraw-Hill

Shushan, Gregory (2009): *Conceptions of the Afterlife in Early Civilizations. Universalism, Constructivism, and Near-Death Experience*. London/New York: Continuum

Steiger, Brad; Steiger, Sherry Hansen (2003): *The Gale Encyclopedia of the Unusual and Unexplained*. Detroit u.a.: Thomson Gale

Strassman, Rick (2001): *DMT: The Spirit Molecule. A Doctor's Revolutionary Research into the Biology of Near-Death and Mystical Experiences*. Rochester: Park Street Press

Stutley, Margaret (2003): *Shamanism. An Introduction*. London/New York: Routledge

Tausin, Floco (2012a): "Diagram about Eye Floaters and Other Subjective Visual Phenomena". *Eye-floaters.info.* eye-floaters.info/floaters/subjective-visual-phenomena.htm (19.9.22)

Tausin, Floco (2012b): "Lights from the Other World – Floater Structures in the Visual Arts of Modern and Present-Day Shamans". *Ovi Magazine*, 19.5.12. ovimagazine.com/art/8648 (19.9.22)

Tausin, Floco (2011a): "'Hair standing on end'. Prickle feelings in spirituality and holistic medicine". *The Art of Healing* 3, no. 36.

Tausin, Floco (2011b): "Vitreous opacity vs. nervous system – Do eye floaters arise from the visual nervous system?" *Ovi Magazine*, 31.10.11. ovimagazine.com/art/7852 (19.9.22)

Tausin, Floco (2010a): "Eye Floaters. Floating spheres and strings in a seer's view". *Holistic Vision* 2. eye-floaters.info/news/news-june2010.htm#1 (19.9.22)

Tausin, Floco (2010b): "Entoptic phenomena as universal trance phenomena". *Unexplained Mysteries,* 20.10.10. unexplained-mysteries.com/column.php?id=192724 (19.9.22)

Tausin, Floco (2009): *Mouches Volantes. Eye Floaters as Shining Structure of Consciousness*. Bern: Leuchtstruktur Verlag

Tausin, Floco (2008): "Lesertipp: Mouches volantes und Orbs". *Ganzheitlich Sehen* 3. mouches-volantes.com/news/newsoktober2008.htm#2 (19.9.22)

Tausin, Floco (2007): "Paranormale visuelle Phänomene: Orbs, Aura, Mouches volanets und 'Sternchen' im Vergleich". *Parawelten. Grenzwissenschaften – UFOs – Paraphänomene. Publikation der Interessensgruppe für Grenzwissenschaften & Paraphänomene* 1/2

Van Lommel et al. (2001): "Near-death experience in survivors of cardiac arrest: a prospective study in the Netherlands". *Lancet* 358: 2039-45

Williams, Kevin (2007): "The NDE and Orbs. Kevin William's research conclusions". *Near-Death Experiences and the Afterlife.* near-death.com/science/research/orbs.html (15.10.19)

Williams Cook, Emily; Greyson, Bruce; Stevenson, Ian (1998): "Do any near-death experiences provide evidence for the survival of human personality after death? Relevant features and illustrative case reports". *Journal of Scientific Exploration* 12, no. 3: 377-406

Woofenden, Lee (2009): *Death and Rebirth: From near death experiences to eternal life.* NCE Ministries

Zaleski, Carol (1993): *Nah-Todeserlebnisse und Jenseitsvisionen vom Mittelalter bis zur Gegenwart.* Frankfurt a.M. et al.: Insel Verlag

## Links

Link[1]: *Unexplained-mysteries.com*, 4.11.12. unexplained-mysteries.com/column.php?id=237145 (19.9.22)

Link[2]: commons.wikimedia.org/wiki/File:Paradiso_Canto_31.jpg (19.9.22)

Link[3]: de.wikipedia.org/wiki/Aufstieg_der_Seligen_(Hieronymus_Bosch) (19.9.22)

Link[4]: klarblicker.de/paranormal/durchdaslicht.html (19.1.11)

Link[5]: diggapic.com/pictures/iands.org (19.1.11).

# The Author

**Floco Tausin**

floco.tausin@eye-floaters.info

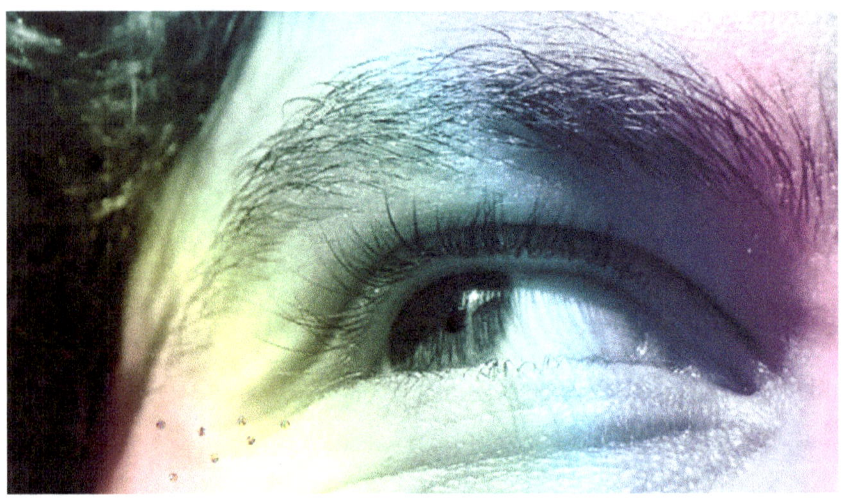

The name Floco Tausin is a pseudonym. The author received a PhD at the Faculty of the Humanities at the University of Bern, Switzerland. In theory and practice he is engaged in the research of subjective visual phenomena in connection with altered states of consciousness and the development of consciousness. In 2009, he published the mystical story Mouches Volantes about the spiritual dimension of eye floaters.

**The book**

*Mouches Volantes. Eye Floaters as Shining Structure of Consciousness*
(Spiritual Fiction. ISBN: 978-3033003378. Paperback, 15.2 x 22.9 cm / 6 x 9 inches, 368 pages).

Floco Tausin tells the story about his time of learning with spiritual teacher and seer Nestor, taking place in the hilly region of Emmental, Switzerland. The mystic teachings focus on the widely known but underestimated dots and strands floating in our field of vision, known as eye floaters or mouches volantes. Whereas in ophthalmology, floaters are considered a harmless vitreous opacity, the author gradually learns to see them and reveals the first emergence of the shining structure formed by our consciousness.

Mouches Volantes explores the topic of eye floaters in a much wider sense than the usual medical explanations. It merges scientific research, esoteric philosophy and practical consciousness development, and observes the spiritual meaning and everyday life implications of these dots and strands.

*Mouches Volantes – a mystical story about the closest thing in the world.*